D1131739

School Shootings and the
Never Again Movement

**Recent Titles in
21st-Century Turning Points**

The #MeToo Movement
Laurie Collier Hillstrom

The NFL National Anthem Protests
Margaret Haerens

School Shootings and the
Never Again Movement

Laurie Collier Hillstrom

21st-Century Turning Points

An Imprint of ABC-CLIO, LLC
Santa Barbara, California • Denver, Colorado

Library of Congress Cataloging-in-Publication Data

Names: Hillstrom, Laurie Collier, 1965- author.
Title: School shootings and the Never Again Movement / Laurie Collier Hillstrom.
Description: Santa Barbara, California : ABC-CLIO, 2019. | Series: 21st-century turning points | Includes bibliographical references and index.
Identifiers: LCCN 2018058140 (print) | LCCN 2018059275 (ebook) | ISBN 9781440867521 (ebook) | ISBN 9781440867514 (cloth : alk. paper)
Subjects: LCSH: School shootings—United States. | Student movements—United States. | Gun control—United States.
Classification: LCC LB3013.32 (ebook) | LCC LB3013.32 .H55 2019 (print) | DDC 371.7/820973—dc23
LC record available at https://lccn.loc.gov/2018058140

ISBN: 978-1-4408-6751-4 (print)
       978-1-4408-6752-1 (ebook)

23 22 21 20 19   1 2 3 4 5

This book is also available as an eBook.

ABC-CLIO
An Imprint of ABC-CLIO, LLC

ABC-CLIO, LLC
147 Castilian Drive
Santa Barbara, California 93117
www.abc-clio.com

This book is printed on acid-free paper ∞

Manufactured in the United States of America

Contents

Series Foreword   vii

Chapter 1   Overview of School Shootings and the Never
              Again Movement   1

Chapter 2   **Landmark Events**   13
              The University of Texas Tower Shooting (1966)   13
              The Gun Control Act (1968)   17
              The NRA Cincinnati Revolt (1977)   21
              The Firearms Owners' Protection Act (1986)   25
              The Brady Bill and Assault Weapons Ban (1993–1994)   29
              The Columbine High School Shooting (1999)   32
              The Virginia Tech Shooting (2007)   38
              District of Columbia v. Heller (2008)   41
              The Sandy Hook Elementary School Shooting (2012)   45
              The Umpqua Community College Shooting (2015)   50
              The Las Vegas Shooting (2017)   52
              The Marjory Stoneman Douglas High School
                  Shooting (2018)   57
              The Never Again Movement Forms (2018)   61
              The March for Our Lives (2018)   66
              The Santa Fe High School Shooting (2018)   73

Chapter 3   **Impacts of the Never Again Movement**   77
              The March for Our Lives Demands   77
              School Safety and Proposals to Arm Teachers   91
              A New Age of Youth Activism   96
              A Shift in Public Sentiments about Gun Control   102

Chapter 4   **Profiles**   109
            Mark Barden (1965?–)   109
            Gun violence prevention advocate and
            cofounder of Sandy Hook Promise
            Michael Bloomberg (1942–)   112
            Former mayor of New York City and
            cofounder of Everytown for Gun Safety
            Jaclyn Corin (2000–)   115
            Parkland school shooting survivor and
            March for Our Lives organizer
            Gabby Giffords (1970–)   118
            Former U.S. representative from Arizona,
            gun violence victim, and gun safety advocate
            Emma González (1999–)   121
            Parkland school shooting survivor and gun
            control advocate
            Nicole Hockley (1970?–)   125
            Gun violence prevention expert and cofounder
            of Sandy Hook Promise
            David Hogg (2000–)   128
            Parkland school shooting survivor and gun
            control advocate
            Cameron Kasky (2000–)   130
            Parkland school shooting survivor and
            cofounder of Never Again MSD
            Wayne LaPierre (1949–)   133
            Gun rights activist and chief executive officer
            of the National Rifle Association
            Dana Loesch (1978–)   136
            Conservative talk show host and national spokesperson
            for the National Rifle Association
            Shannon Watts (1971–)   139
            Gun control activist and founder of Moms Demand
            Action for Gun Sense in America

Further Resources   143

Index   149

Series Foreword

21st-Century Turning Points is a general reference series that has been crafted for use by high school and undergraduate students as well as members of the general public. The purpose of the series is to give readers a clear, authoritative, and unbiased understanding of major fast-breaking events, movements, people, and issues that are transforming American life, culture, and politics in this turbulent new century. Each volume constitutes a one-stop resource for learning about a single issue or event currently dominating America's news headlines and political discussions—issues or events that, in many cases, are also driving national debate about our country's leaders, institutions, values, and priorities.

Each volume in the *21st-Century Turning Points* series begins with an **Overview** of the event or issue that is the subject of the book. It then provides a suite of informative chronologically arranged narrative entries on specific **Landmarks** in the evolution of the event or issue in question. This chapter provides both vital historical context and insights into present-day news events to give readers a full and clear understanding of how current issues and controversies evolved.

The next chapter of the book is devoted to examining the **Impacts** of the event or issue in question on various aspects of American life, including political, economic, cultural, and interpersonal implications. It is followed by a chapter of biographical **Profiles** that summarize the life experiences and personal beliefs of prominent individuals associated with the event or issue in question.

Finally, each book concludes with a topically-organized **Further Resources** list of important and informative resources—from influential books to fascinating websites—to which readers can turn for additional information, and a carefully compiled subject **Index**.

These complementary elements, found in every book in the series, work together to create an evenhanded, authoritative, and user-friendly tool for gaining a deeper and more accurate understanding of the fast-changing nation in which we live—and the issues and moments that define us as we move deeper into the twenty-first century.

CHAPTER ONE

Overview of School Shootings and the Never Again Movement

Issues surrounding gun rights and gun control provoke contentious debates in the United States. Gun rights supporters argue that the Second Amendment to the U.S. Constitution grants individual citizens a fundamental right to possess guns without government interference. They resist most proposed regulations on firearms, claiming that gun control laws infringe upon the rights of law-abiding gun owners while doing nothing to prevent criminals from gaining access to weapons. Gun control advocates, on the other hand, argue that the widespread availability of guns has contributed to an epidemic of gun violence in the United States. They contend that strict new laws are needed to prevent dangerous people from obtaining firearms and to protect innocent lives. The opposing sides in this debate are locked in a perpetual struggle that has prevented major changes to the nation's gun laws for decades.

Mass shootings—and especially school shootings—have intensified public concerns about the prevalence of gun violence in the twenty-first century. These unpredictable, senseless acts have left many Americans feeling vulnerable and afraid for the safety of their families. Yet rising apprehension following mass shootings at schools, concert venues, nightclubs, office buildings, shopping malls, and churches has not prompted reform of federal gun laws. Efforts to pass gun control legislation are consistently defeated by staunch opposition from the vocal and well-financed gun lobby, led by the National Rifle Association (NRA) and its 5 million members. "This has become an American routine: After every mass shooting, the debate over guns and gun violence starts up once again," German Lopez wrote in Vox. "Maybe some bills get introduced. Critics respond with concerns that the government is trying to take away their guns. The debate stalls. So even as America continues experiencing levels of gun violence unrivaled in the rest of the developed world, nothing happens—no laws are passed by Congress, nothing significant is done to try to prevent the next horror" (Lopez 2018b).

On February 14, 2018, a gunman armed with an AR-15–style semiautomatic rifle walked into Marjory Stoneman Douglas (MSD) High School in Parkland, Florida, and murdered 17 students and staff members. For the teenagers who hid in closets, cowered under desks, jumped out of windows, ran terrified through hallways, or administered first aid to bleeding classmates, life would never be the same again. Going through the trauma of a school shooting, and seeing their friends and teachers killed, made the endless gun debate seem absurd. "What matters is that the majority of American people have become complacent in a senseless injustice that occurs all around them," said MSD senior Emma González. "What matters is that most American politicians have become more easily swayed by money than by the people who voted them into office. What matters is that my friends are dead, along with hundreds upon hundreds of others all over the United States" (González 2018).

In the days and weeks after the MSD shooting, González and other student survivors emerged at the forefront of a powerful new youth-led movement demanding gun reform. Describing themselves as members of the "mass shooting generation," the teenage activists expressed outrage at the legislative inaction that had failed to keep them safe from gun violence at school. Through media appearances, town hall meetings, rallies, speeches, and a social media campaign using the hashtag #NeverAgain, the Parkland students galvanized a generation of young people to counteract the political influence of the NRA. The clearest indication that the MSD shooting might prove to be a tipping point in the long, contentious debate over gun control took place on March 24, 2018, when more than 2 million people joined in the nationwide March for Our Lives protest against gun violence.

Although it remains to be seen whether the Never Again movement can achieve its goal of reforming America's gun laws, supporters note that the 90 million millennials of voting age will make up nearly 40 percent of the U.S. electorate by 2020 (Hansen 2018). The Parkland activists' long-term strategy involves using the collective voting power of their generation to elect leaders who share their commitment to enacting meaningful gun control legislation. "If you listen real close, you can hear the people in power shaking. They've gotten used to being protective of their position, the safety of inaction. Inaction is no longer safe," MSD senior David Hogg declared at the March for Our Lives. "To those politicians that say change will not come, I say: We will not stop until every man, every woman, every child, and every American can live without fear of gun violence" (Hogg 2018).

Guns and Gun Violence in the United States

The United States has the highest rate of private gun ownership in the world, with 120.5 firearms per 100 residents as of 2017. Americans own almost 50 percent of all guns in civilian hands worldwide, even though they make up less than 5 percent of the world's total population (Lopez 2018b). A 2017 Pew Research Center survey found that gun ownership was concentrated among a minority of citizens. Around 30 percent of adults said that they currently owned a gun, while 57 percent reported living in a household without guns. The survey found the highest rates of gun ownership among white men living in rural areas who expressed a political affiliation with the Republican Party. Among gun owners, two-thirds reported having multiple guns, while three-quarters described the possession of firearms as an essential component of their personal freedom (Igielnik and Brown 2017).

Gun violence is a significant problem in the United States. Firearms killed more than 37,000 Americans in 2016, or about 100 people per day. The U.S. death rate from gun violence, at 10.6 per 100,000 population, is the highest of any developed country (Lopez 2018a). In fact, Americans' risk of being shot to death is 25 times greater than that faced by citizens of other high-income nations (Pahn, Knopov, and Siegel 2018). The prevalence of gun violence is particularly high among young Americans. In fact, firearms were the leading cause of death for young men between the ages of 15 and 19 in 2016, accounting for 30 percent of all deaths (Pane 2018).

Although mass shootings receive a great deal of media attention, they account for less than 2 percent of all U.S. deaths from gun violence. The Gun Violence Archive defines a mass shooting as a distinct event in which four or more people, excluding the shooter, are shot in the same general location and time period. Using this definition, the organization reported that 346 mass shootings occurred in 2017, resulting in 437 deaths and 1,802 injuries (Mosher and Gould 2018). The Federal Bureau of Investigation (FBI) defines an active-shooter incident as one in which an individual uses a firearm in a populated area to kill or attempt to kill multiple people. Applying this stricter definition, the FBI designated 50 shootings that occurred in 2016 and 2017—including 7 that took place in schools—as active-shooter incidents, resulting in 221 deaths and 722 injuries (Federal Bureau of Investigation 2018). Even though mass shootings are relatively rare, intensive media coverage extends the psychological and emotional impact of these traumatic incidents far beyond the individuals and communities directly affected by them (Cox and Rich 2018).

Gun owners and non–gun owners tend to hold different views of the severity and causes of gun violence in the United States. Nearly 60 percent of non–gun owners describe gun violence as a major problem in American society, and two-thirds say that easy access to legal firearms contributes to its prevalence. In contrast, only one-third of gun owners see gun violence as a big problem, while 44 percent view the availability of firearms as a contributing factor (Igielnik and Brown 2017). These differing perspectives lead to disagreements over gun control laws and whether they are effective means of reducing gun violence. Nevertheless, research has revealed a strong public consensus around some proposed changes to the nation's gun laws. A 2017 Pew survey, for example, found that more than three-quarters of both Democrats and Republicans favored universal background checks on gun purchases (Lopez 2018c).

Gun Rights and the Second Amendment

Even gun control measures that enjoy broad popular support, however, encounter opposition from the NRA. The NRA emerged as a political lobbying force in 1977, after a group of hard-line gun rights activists took over leadership of the organization at its annual meeting in Cincinnati, Ohio. The new leaders promoted the view that the Second Amendment conveys an individual right to bear arms rather than a collective right in connection with service in a state militia. They asserted that citizens have a responsibility to arm themselves and defend their rights against potential acts of repression by a tyrannical government. They also claimed that allowing any government regulation of firearms would open the door to an eventual ban on civilian gun ownership and the confiscation of guns from private citizens. Adopting these views, some Americans came to regard gun ownership as an important duty and an essential element of their identity and culture.

Over time, an increasing number of Americans accepted the NRA's position on gun ownership as an individual right. A series of Gallup polls showed that public support for the concept of banning the possession of handguns except by law enforcement declined steadily from 60 percent in 1959, to 38 percent in 1980, to 23 percent in 2016 (Lopez 2018c). As the NRA intensified its lobbying efforts, the organization became more closely aligned with the Republican Party, which added progun planks to its national platform. Polls showed a marked increase in Republican support for protecting individual gun ownership rights, from 45 percent in 1993 to 79 percent in 2017 (C. K. 2018). Meanwhile, the Democratic Party made gun control one of its main priorities, and support for firearm regulation grew among Democrats. In 2008, the U.S. Supreme Court codified the NRA's interpretation of the Second Amendment in *District of Columbia v. Heller.* According to gun control advocates, the court's formal recognition of an individual right to bear arms had a legal, political, and psychological impact that made it more difficult to pass commonsense gun laws.

Today, the NRA stands as one of the most influential forces in American politics. The organization has devoted vast sums of money to campaign contributions and issue advertising, mobilized its members to vote, and applied pressure through lobbying efforts and media campaigns to convince lawmakers to support its agenda. In addition to adopting a no-compromise approach toward gun control proposals, NRA leaders also actively pursue legislation to expand gun rights. They fight to eliminate restrictions on concealed weapons, for instance, to allow gun owners to carry firearms into schools, churches, bars, and sporting events. They also promote the idea that having more guns in more places increases public safety by deterring crime and keeping the peace.

Although the NRA's staunch defense of gun rights inspires its members, some of its tactics have alienated people with more mainstream views on gun issues. "The NRA has made a deliberate choice to take a very extreme, hardline approach when it comes to the issue of gun violence and has become increasingly more extreme in its messaging," said Chelsea Parsons of the Center for American Progress. "That hyper-extreme messaging is really not resonating with a majority of Americans, who are sick and tired of the gun violence problem in this country. They're looking for solutions and prevention, and that's not what you get from the NRA" (Bonazzo 2018).

Mass Shootings and Demands for Action

Public outrage about gun violence, along with demands for stricter gun control laws, typically spikes following mass shootings in the United States. As the frequency of mass shootings increased in the twenty-first century, many Americans felt under siege from a steady barrage of gun violence. Several of the deadliest mass shootings in U.S. history occurred within an 18-month period in 2016 and 2017. On June 12, 2016, a gunman killed 49 people at a gay nightclub in Orlando, Florida. On October 1, 2017, a sniper fired on the crowd at an open-air country music festival in Las Vegas, Nevada, killing 58 people and wounding 400 others. Just over a month later, a gunman killed 26 worshipers in a Baptist church outside of San Antonio, Texas.

Many mass shooting events have taken place at schools. Since the 1999 shooting at Columbine High School in Littleton, Colorado, school shootings have occurred an average of 10 times per year in the United States (Cox and Rich 2018). The second-deadliest school shooting in U.S. history occurred on December 14, 2012, when a gunman murdered 26 students and educators at Sandy Hook Elementary School in Newtown, Connecticut. Twenty of the victims were first-grade students between six and seven years old. Many observers thought that the horrific events in Newtown would break the pattern of political inaction. President Barack Obama, whose two terms in office were marked by 14 mass shootings, demanded that Congress pass legislation to ban assault weapons and require universal background checks. "No single law—no set of laws—can eliminate evil from the world, or prevent every senseless act of violence in our society. But that can't be an excuse for inaction," he stated. "Are we really prepared to say that we're powerless in the face of such carnage, that the politics are too hard? Are we prepared to say that such violence visited on our children year after year after year is somehow the price of our freedom?" (Marcin 2017).

The parents of several Sandy Hook victims also emerged as leading voices calling for gun control. Grief, anger, and frustration over the shooting led to the creation of new organizations dedicated to gun violence prevention, including Sandy Hook Promise and Moms Demand Action for Gun Sense in America. Public opinion polls in the aftermath of Newtown showed that a majority of Americans favored gun control over gun rights for the first time in Obama's presidency. Yet the NRA launched a $10 million opposition campaign that succeeded in blocking the proposed gun control legislation. At the same time, the nation's gun dealers set a record with 2.2 million firearm sales in the month after the Newtown shooting. "It's not the actual event of the mass shooting that causes people to be concerned about their firearm rights as they understand them. It's what happens after the shooting," explained economist Jurgen Brauer. "Whenever there is a threat of legislation, either at the state level or at the federal level, then people run into the firearm stores and purchase more guns" (Keneally 2016).

Although Columbine, Sandy Hook, and other school shootings did not result in gun reform, they did convince countless schools across the United States to adopt new security measures aimed at preventing shootings. Such measures—which include fortifying school buildings, hiring armed security guards and resource officers, implementing lockdown procedures and active-shooter drills, and establishing emergency notification systems—fundamentally changed the educational experiences of a generation of American students. Children in the mass shooting generation learned to remain vigilant at all times. For some students, the extreme measures taken to promote school safety create a perception of danger that causes psychological trauma and inhibits learning. In a nationwide survey of teenagers conducted in 2018, 57 percent said they were worried about the possibility of a shooting happening at their school, while only 13 percent said they were not at all worried (Graf 2018).

Gun rights supporters argue that mass shootings are too rare to use as the basis for making wholesale changes to the nation's gun laws. "We treasure our personal freedoms in America, and unfortunately, occasional mass shootings, as horrific as they are, is one of the prices that we pay for the freedoms that we enjoy," said criminologist James Alan Fox (Follman 2014). Gun control advocates, on the other hand, contend that mass shootings are symptomatic of the larger crisis surrounding gun violence in the United States. They point out that children in other developed countries do not have to worry about being shot at school. A CNN analysis found that 288 shootings occurred at schools and colleges in the United States between 2009 and 2018, while the other G7 advanced nations experienced 5 school shootings combined (Grabow and Rose 2018).

The Never Again Movement and the March for Our Lives

By the time the MSD shooting occurred in early 2018, just a few months after the deadly mass shootings in Las Vegas and Texas, such incidents had come to seem commonplace to many Americans. Few people expected that the outcome of this school shooting would be any different than the ones that had come before. Most anticipated that the latest tragedy would fade from the headlines without inspiring political action beyond the usual "thoughts and prayers" from state and federal lawmakers. As soon as the student survivors of the Parkland shooting were forced into the national spotlight, however, it became clear that they planned to use their platform to promote change. They gave interviews, delivered speeches, participated in a televised CNN town hall, met with state lawmakers, and organized the National School Walkout. Many students focused their anger on the political influence wielded by the NRA. They shamed law-makers for valuing NRA campaign funds over the lives of children, and they compiled a list of demands for gun control legislation.

The MSD students formed a political action committee, Never Again MSD, and organized a social media campaign using the hashtag #Never-Again. The name represented their promise to continue fighting for gun reform to ensure that a massacre such as the one that took the lives of their friends would never happen again at another school. By appealing to young people who had grown up in an age of gun violence and school shootings, the Never Again activists mobilized an equivalent force to the NRA on the gun control side of the debate. The student-led March for Our Lives was one of the largest protest demonstrations in U.S. history. To turn their message into political action, the Parkland survivors empha-sized registering young voters, encouraging civic participation, and turn-ing gun control into a key voting issue for their generation. "We will get rid of these public servants that only serve the gun lobby," Hogg declared, "and we will save lives" (Hogg 2018).

The Never Again movement met with a great deal of criticism and con-tempt from gun rights supporters. Some conservative commentators called the teenage activists names, questioned their motives for speaking out, or claimed that they were too young to understand the complexities of the gun debate. Some right-wing media personalities attempted to dis-credit the Parkland students by promoting conspiracy theories claiming that they were "crisis actors" hired by powerful antigun forces seeking to exploit the tragedy for political gain. On the day of the March for Our Lives, the NRA posted the following message on Facebook: "Today's pro-tests aren't spontaneous. Gun-hating billionaires and Hollywood elites are manipulating and exploiting children as part of their plan to DESTROY the Second Amendment and strip us of our right to defend ourselves and our loved ones" (National Rifle Association 2018). Never Again leaders fought back against their critics on social media with a combination of sarcastic comebacks and viral campaigns calling for consumer boycotts of companies that advertised on conservative talk shows or provided dis-counts to NRA members.

The Parkland students' gun reform advocacy prompted a shift in public opinion, with polls conducted after the March for Our Lives showing that two-thirds of Americans favor stricter firearms regulation—the highest level of support for gun control since passage of the Brady Handgun Vio-lence Prevention Act in 1993 (C. K. 2018). The Never Again activists' cam-paign to register and energize young voters also proved effective. Surveys found that 31 percent of Americans between the ages of 18 and 29 cast ballots in the November 2018 midterm elections, an increase of 10 points over 2014 and the highest level of participation in nearly three decades (Hansen 2018).

Although the MSD students recognize that social change is a long-term process, they also know that the young people of their generation are the leaders and policy makers of the future. "We understand that we are just kids and we understand that all of our demands might not become reality for a while, but we will not let them win," said MSD junior Jaclyn Corin. "We will not let the perpetrators of mass shootings win. We will not let the National Rifle Association and its supporters win. . . . We are doing this for us. We are doing this for the victims of Columbine, Sandy Hook, and every other mass shooting. But most of all we are fighting for your kids and the kids of the future so they don't grow up with the constant fear of getting shot at school, church, the movie theater, or a concert. We, the mass shooting generation, will stop at nothing to make our voices be heard and our wishes a reality" (Corin 2018).

Further Reading

Bonazzo, John. 2018. "NRA Slipping with Voters, though Many Have Moved On from Gun Control." *Observer,* September 10, 2018. https://observer.com /2018/09/nra-gun-control-polling-parkland/.

C. K. 2018. "Gun Politics after Parkland: Has Anything Changed?" *The Economist,* May 3, 2018. https://www.economist.com/democracy-in-america/2018/05 /02/gun-politics-after-parkland.

Corin, Jaclyn. 2018. "With the March for Our Lives, We Are Fighting for Your Kids." *Sun-Sentinel,* March 19, 2018. https://www.sun-sentinel.com/opin ion/commentary/fl-op-viewpoint-jaclyn-corin-speech-march-for-our -lives-20180319-story.html.

Cox, John Woodrow, and Steven Rich. 2018. "Scarred by School Shootings." *Washington Post,* March 25, 2018. https://www.washingtonpost.com /graphics/2018/local/us-school-shootings-history/?utm_term=.311 d4c0661d5.

Federal Bureau of Investigation. 2018. "Active Shooter Incidents in the United States in 2016 and 2017." U.S. Department of Justice, April 2018. https://www.fbi .gov/file-repository/active-shooter-incidents-us-2016-2017.pdf/view.

Follman, Mark. 2014. "Yes, Mass Shootings Are Occurring More Often." *Mother Jones,* October 21, 2014. https://www.motherjones.com/politics/2014/10 /mass-shootings-rising-harvard/.

González, Emma. 2018. "Parkland Student Emma González Opens Up about Her Fight for Gun Control." *Harper's Bazaar,* February 26, 2018. https:// www.harpersbazaar.com/culture/politics/a18715714/protesting-nra-gun -control-true-story/.

Grabow, Chip, and Lisa Rose. 2018. "The U.S. Has Had 57 Times as Many School Shootings as the Other Major Industrialized Nations Combined." CNN, May 18, 2018. https://www.cnn.com/2018/05/21/us/school-shooting-us -versus-world-trnd/index.html.

Graf, Nikki. 2018. "A Majority of U.S. Teens Fear a Shooting Could Happen at Their School, and Most Parents Share Their Concern." Pew Research Center, April 18, 2018. http://www.pewresearch.org/fact-tank/2018/04/18/a -majority-of-u-s-teens-fear-a-shooting-could-happen-at-their-school-and -most-parents-share-their-concern/.

Hansen, Claire. 2018. "Young Voters Turned Out in Historic Numbers, Early Estimates Show." *U.S. News and World Report,* November 7, 2018. https://www .usnews.com/news/politics/articles/2018-11-07/young-voters-turned -out-in-historic-numbers-early-estimates-show.

Hogg, David. 2018. "March for Our Lives: Stoneman Douglas Student David Hogg's Speech." NBC News, March 24, 2018. https://www.nbcnews.com /video/march-for-our-lives-stoneman-douglas-student-david-hogg-s -speech-1194238019932?v=railb&.

Igielnik, Ruth, and Anna Brown. 2017. "Key Takeaways on Americans' Views of Guns and Gun Ownership." Pew Research Center, June 22, 2017. http:// www.pewresearch.org/fact-tank/2017/06/22/key-takeaways-on -americans-views-of-guns-and-gun-ownership/.

Keneally, Meghan. 2016. "Four Years after Sandy Hook, Obama Leaves a Legacy of Little Progress on Gun Laws." ABC News, December 14, 2016. https:// abcnews.go.com/Politics/years-sandy-hook-obama-leaves-legacy-progr ess-gun/story?id=44163755.

Lopez, German. 2017. "How the NRA Resurrected the Second Amendment." Vox, October 12, 2017. https://www.vox.com/policy-and-politics/2017/10 /12/16418524/nra-second-amendment-guns-violence.

Lopez, German. 2018a. "America Is One of Six Countries That Make Up More Than Half of Gun Deaths Worldwide." Vox, August 28, 2018. https:// www.vox.com/2018/8/29/17792776/us-gun-deaths-global.

Lopez, German. 2018b. "America's Gun Problem, Explained." Vox, November 8, 2018. https://www.vox.com/2015/10/3/9444417/gun-violence-united-states -america.

Lopez, German. 2018c. "Why the March for Our Lives Could Win." Vox, March 26, 2018. https://www.vox.com/policy-and-politics/2018/3/24/17158592 /march-for-our-lives-gun-control-nra.

Marcin, Tim. 2017. "Trump Supported Obama's Sandy Hook Response Calling for Gun Control." *Newsweek,* October 2, 2017. https://www.newsweek .com/trump-supported-obama-sandy-hook-massacre-response-calling -gun-control-675369.

Mosher, Dave, and Skye Gould. 2018. "The Odds That a Gun Will Kill the Average American May Surprise You." Business Insider, October 29, 2018. https://www.businessinsider.com/us-gun-death-murder-risk-statistics -2018-3.

National Rifle Association. 2018. "#WhatIf." Facebook, March 24, 2018. https://www.facebook.com/NRA/videos/2121233114561375/.

Pahn, Molly, Anita Knopov, and Michael Siegel. 2018. "Gun Violence in the U.S. Kills More Black People and Urban Dwellers." The Conversation, November 8, 2018. http://theconversation.com/gun-violence-in-the-us-kills-more-black-people-and-urban-dwellers-86825.

Pane, Natalia E. 2018. "Data Point: Gun Violence Is the Most Common Cause of Death for Young Men." Child Trends, February 22, 2018. https://www.childtrends.org/gun-violence-common-cause-death-young-men.

CHAPTER TWO

Landmark Events

This chapter explores important milestones and events in the debate over gun control and gun rights in the United States. It charts the expanding political influence of the National Rifle Association, the growing public concern about school shootings following the tragedies at Columbine and Sandy Hook, and the long legislative impasse over proposed measures to prevent gun violence. It then traces the launch of the Never Again movement by student survivors of the Parkland shooting, culminating in the 2018 March for Our Lives protest.

The University of Texas Tower Shooting (1966)

Some historians date the beginning of the era of U.S. school shootings to August 1, 1966. On that day—long before the media coined such terms as "mass shooting" and "active shooter"—a gunman climbed to the top of the clock tower at the University of Texas at Austin (UT) and opened fire on the campus below. By the time police officers killed the shooter 96 minutes later, the rampage had taken the lives of 13 people and injured 31 others. "It was a seminal event, the first of its kind," said Gary Lavergne, who chronicled the shooting in his book *A Sniper in the Tower* (1997). "It kind of defines for us what is a mass murder" (Tolson 2016). The UT shooting led to a revolution in how law enforcement responded to crisis situations, launched a national debate about gun control, and created a new sense of vulnerability to random acts of violence in public spaces.

The Incident

The perpetrator of the UT tower shooting, 25-year-old Charles Whitman, had trained as a sharpshooter in the U.S. Marine Corps before enrolling at UT to study architectural engineering. He struggled in his studies, abused amphetamines, and told a therapist on campus that he experienced severe headaches and overwhelming violent impulses, including recurring thoughts about taking a rifle to the top of the tower. Since the therapist had treated many other students who mentioned violent fantasies, he did not view Whitman's statement as a threat. "Today we take it a whole lot more seriously because of our history," Lavergne noted. "But back then, that kind of thing didn't happen" (Silverman 2016).

Sometime during the night of July 31, 1966, Whitman killed his mother, Margaret, and his wife, Kathleen, by stabbing them as they slept. In notes left with their bodies, he explained that he wanted to spare them humiliation and suffering. The next morning Whitman rented a dolly, visited several stores to purchase guns and ammunition, dressed up as a maintenance man, and drove to the Main Building on the UT campus. He packed seven guns into a footlocker and placed food and other supplies into a duffel bag, loaded them on the dolly, and rode the elevator up the tower. The prominent structure was the tallest building in Austin. In addition to containing offices and classrooms, it featured a four-sided observation deck 230 feet above street level that offered students and tourists an excellent view of the campus, the city, and the surrounding Hill Country.

Upon reaching the 27th-floor lobby, Whitman killed the receptionist who checked in visitors and hid her body behind a sofa. He then shot several members of a family on the stairs that led to the observation deck. At 11:48 a.m., Whitman positioned himself on the deck and began shooting at people below. His first target was Claire Williams, a pregnant student who sustained a gunshot wound to the abdomen as she walked across the South Mall with her boyfriend. Although Williams survived, her unborn baby and her boyfriend were killed. Other victims included students, university employees, and visitors walking through campus or patronizing the shops and restaurants along Guadalupe Street. The carnage eventually spanned a five-block radius, with some people hit up to 500 yards away from the base of the tower.

At first, no one on the ground seemed to understand what was happening. Some witnesses attributed the loud sounds to a nearby construction project, while others thought that the people yelling, running, or falling down around them were taking part in an antiwar protest or a theatrical performance. When someone finally called the police to report a sniper in the tower, the response was slow and disorganized. The university did not have its own police force at that time, and the Austin Police Department did not have a tactical response unit. The first officers on the scene were armed with service revolvers or shotguns, which lacked the range to reach the top of the tower, and their communication was limited to a few hand-held radios and an overwhelmed landline phone system. "It was like a ship without a rudder," said Ramiro Martinez, an off-duty officer who rushed to the scene from his home after hearing news reports of the shootings. "Leadership broke down that day as far as I'm concerned" (Haurwitz 2016).

In the absence of a visible police presence, some students and pass-ersby took matters into their own hands. Some people blocked intersec-tions or building exits to prevent others from getting into the line of fire. Rescuers risked their own lives by running into the open to drag shooting victims to safety. Some locals retrieved hunting rifles from nearby apart-ments and vehicles and fired at the tower from behind trees. "I hadn't fully comprehended that lots of people around me in Austin not only owned guns but had them close at hand and regarded themselves as free to use them," said Nobel Prize–winning novelist J. M. Coetzee, who attended UT on a Fulbright scholarship at that time (Colloff 2006). Although some wit-nesses claimed that the gunfire helped the situation by distracting the sniper and forcing him to take cover, others argued that the vigilantism added to the chaos and made the situation more dangerous, especially for first responders.

When Martinez reached campus, he ran across the South Mall to the tower, zigzagging between dead and injured people on the ground. "It was traumatic, you just had to keep going," he recalled. "I figured the best thing to do would be to get inside of the Tower. . . . I had a very simple plan that day, and it was to kill the sniper or be killed. I had to stop him from hurt-ing other people" (Cardenas 2016). Another Austin Police Department offi-cer, Houston McCoy, arrived at the tower a few minutes later. Upon taking the elevator to the top, the men expected to find a police command post, with leaders formulating a plan to apprehend the shooter. Instead, they encountered only one other officer, Jerry Day, and a civilian volunteer, Allen Crum. While Crum stood guard and Day escorted students and pro-fessors who had been trapped in classrooms out of the building, Martinez and McCoy climbed to the observation deck and confronted the sniper. Both officers fired their weapons, and the shooting rampage ended with Whitman's death at 1:24 p.m.

The Aftermath

As the first incident of its kind in the United States, the UT tower shooting received extensive media coverage. Many Americans expressed grief, outrage, and disbelief at the sudden and shocking murders of more than a dozen people as they went about their daily routines on a peaceful college campus. The event shattered the collective sense of confidence and security that most people felt in public spaces and replaced it with new feelings of uncertainty, vulnerability, and fear. Such feelings only increased during the social upheaval of the late 1960s and 1970s, characterized by antiwar protests, civil rights marches, urban riots, and the assassination of several prominent public figures.

The UT shooting also raised difficult issues that have continued to be debated in the decades since, especially as the frequency of school shootings have increased in the twenty-first century. Many analysts mentioned Whitman's mental health problems and questioned whether better diagnosis and treatment might have prevented him from acting on his violent impulses. An autopsy revealed the presence of a small tumor in Whitman's brain, and some experts claimed that its size and position could have contributed to personality changes, including increased aggression and decreased impulse control. Other experts pointed to Whitman's methodical planning in the hours leading up to the attack as evidence that the tumor had little impact on his decision making or behavior. They also noted that only about 4 percent of violence in the United States was attributable to mental illness. "We know that people with serious mental disorders are at somewhat elevated risk of committing violence," said psychiatric researcher Paul Appelbaum. "Even so, the vast majority of them never commit a violent act" (Silverman 2016).

The UT shooting also prompted a reassessment of police training and response in cities nationwide. In an effort to prepare for future active-shooter situations, many law enforcement agencies created teams of officers with advanced training in the use of special weapons and tactics (SWAT). These rapid-deployment SWAT teams used military-grade equipment and strategies to aggressively confront and subdue snipers and other threats to public safety. Some criminal justice experts claimed that the availability of SWAT teams reduced the need for civilians to participate in the response to an active shooter, as many UT students and Austin residents had by firing their own weapons at the tower sniper. Although some observers claimed that the civilian gunfire reduced the loss of life by suppressing Whitman's ability to track targets on the ground, others argued that this easily could have increased the death toll through friendly fire that missed its target or through misidentification of gun-carrying civilians or plainclothes officers as criminals.

In 2016, the Republican-controlled Texas legislature passed a controversial state law eliminating some restrictions on carrying concealed handguns on college campuses. Although a 1995 law allowed holders of concealed handgun licenses to carry guns on the grounds of public colleges and universities, the new legislation expanded it to allow concealed weapons inside all campus buildings except those specifically designated as gun-exclusion areas by the president of each institution. The law took effect on August 1—the 50th anniversary of the UT tower shooting—and generated vocal opposition on the UT campus. "The fact that it is coming into effect on the 50th anniversary of Charles Whitman has a resonance with a lot of people," said UT law professor Steen Goode, "and serves to heighten for a lot of people a sense of what guns on campus can be, and the harm that guns on campus can do" (Haurwitz 2016). A panel of faculty and students called on university administrators to ban guns from student dormitories, sports venues, faculty offices, and other campus locations.

Further Reading

Akers, Monte, Nathan Akers, and Roger Friedman. 2016. *Tower Sniper: The Terror of America's First Campus Active Shooter.* Houston: John M. Hardy Publishing.

Cardenas, Cat. 2016. "Austin Police Officer Ramiro Martinez Remembers Feeling Sense of Duty to Stop Whitman." *Daily Texan,* August 1, 2016. http://www.dailytexanonline.com/2016/08/01/austin-police-officer-ramiro-martinez-remembers-feeling-sense-of-duty-to-stop-whitman.

Colloff, Pamela. 2006. "96 Minutes." *Texas Monthly,* August 2006. https://www.texasmonthly.com/articles/96-minutes/.

Haurwitz, Ralph K. M. 2016. "How the 1966 Tower Sniper Attack Fueled Debate over Campus Carry at UT." *Austin American-Statesman,* July 7, 2016. https://www.mystatesman.com/news/local/how-the-1966-tower-sniper-attack-fueled-debate-over-campus-carry/VVT2poX9J06zmxlmIBF22K/.

Lavergne, Gary M. 1997. *A Sniper in the Tower: The Charles Whitman Murders.* Denton: University of North Texas Press.

Silverman, Lauren. 2016. "Gun Violence and Mental Health Laws, 50 Years after the Texas Tower Sniper." National Public Radio, July 29, 2016. https://www.npr.org/sections/health-shots/2016/07/29/487767127/gun-violence-and-mental-health-laws-50-years-after-texas-tower-sniper.

Tolson, Mike. 2016. "A Sniper's Haunting Legacy." *Houston Chronicle,* July 30, 2016. https://www.houstonchronicle.com/news/houston-texas/houston/article/A-sniper-s-haunting-legacy-Mass-shooting-in-8774084.php.

The Gun Control Act (1968)

The federal government's authority to regulate guns stems from the constitutional powers granted to Congress to oversee interstate commerce and levy taxes on goods and services. Since the U.S. Constitution leaves most matters relating to police and public safety to the states, federal lawmakers cannot impose gun control measures on that basis. The first federal legislative effort to regulate guns came during Franklin D. Roosevelt's administration with the passage of the National Firearms Act of 1934. In response to a surge in organized crime, the law placed a $200 tax on the manufacture, sale, and transport of machine guns, sawed-off shotguns, silencers, and other weapons commonly used by gangsters such as Al Capone, Pretty Boy Floyd, and Baby Face Nelson. A few years later, the Federal Firearms Act of 1938 required anyone seeking to import, manufacture, or sell guns to obtain a federal license. The law also required gun dealers to keep records of sales and made it illegal to sell guns to convicted felons. Following this brief flurry of gun control measures enacted during the New Deal era, however, the federal government did not address gun control again for three decades.

The Debate over Gun Control

Public calls for congressional action increased during the turbulent 1960s, a period that saw a surge in violent crime in the United States. In 1963, shock and outrage surrounding the assassination of President John F. Kennedy prompted vocal demands for new gun regulations. Democratic senator Thomas J. Dodd of Connecticut introduced a bill focused on limiting the availability of mail-order guns, such as the military-style rifle Lee Harvey Oswald used to murder the president. The bill encountered stiff opposition from members of the National Rifle Association (NRA), though, and failed to advance out of the Senate Commerce Committee. In 1966, following a mass shooting on the campus of the University of Texas at Austin, Dodd renewed his calls for stronger gun control laws. "How many times will we stand witness to such atrocities before we act?" he demanded in a speech. "How many more people must die before the American public, the federal government and the Congress call in unison for effective firearms legislation?" (Westcott 2016).

President Lyndon B. Johnson, a Democrat from Texas who had supported gun control since taking office, made the passage of new gun regulations a top priority for his administration in 1968, following the assassinations of civil rights leader Martin Luther King Jr. and former U.S. attorney general Robert F. Kennedy. On June 6 of that year Johnson signed the Omnibus Safe Streets and Crime Control Act, which included provisions banning the interstate shipment of handguns to individual purchasers and prohibiting individuals from buying handguns outside their state of residence. Johnson continued to press the issue in a message to Congress dated June 24. He noted that the United States ranked worst among industrialized nations for homicides by gunfire at 2.7 per 100,000 population, compared to 0.03 in the Netherlands, 0.04 in Japan, and 0.05 in Great Britain (Johnson 1968a). Johnson called for strong new legislation to reduce crime by halting imports of military surplus and nonsporting guns, ending mail-order weapon purchases, and denying gun access to felons, minors, and persons with mental health issues.

Johnson argued that effective legislation must also include a national system of gun registration and owner licensing. "Registration and licensing have long been an accepted part of daily life in America. Autos, boats, and even dogs and bicycles are commonly registered. Our citizens must get licenses to keep dogs and other pets, to fish, to drive a car," he stated. "Certainly no less should be required for the possession of lethal weapons that have caused so much heartbreak and horror in this country in this century. Surely, the slight inconvenience for the few is minimal when measured against the protection for all" (Johnson 1968a). NRA activists, on the other hand, argued that gun registration requirements violated the Second Amendment. "The federal government has no business maintaining a database or a registration of Americans who are exercising a constitutional right," said NRA lobbyist Chris Cox. "Just like they have no right and no authority to maintain a database of all Methodists, all Baptists, all people of different religious or ethnic backgrounds" (Achenbach, Higham, and Horwitz 2013).

Former astronaut John Glenn, a close friend of the Kennedy family, became head of a bipartisan gun control advocacy group called the Emergency Committee for Gun Control. The organization sought to mobilize Americans who favored gun registration laws to pressure Congress to take action. The committee organized letter-writing campaigns and picket marches and garnered support from dozens of national groups, including the U.S. Chamber of Commerce, the International Association of Chiefs of Police, and the American Civil Liberties Union. The NRA responded with a massive lobbying effort to undermine support for the proposed legislation. NRA leaders warned members that the bill posed a dire threat to the rights of law-abiding citizens to own and use guns, prompting Dodd to accuse the NRA of engaging in "blackmail, intimidation, and unscrupulous propaganda" (Spitzer 1995, 145).

The Law and Its Impact

After months of intense debate, Congress finally passed the Gun Control Act of 1968 (P.L. 90-618, 82 Stat. 1213). When Johnson signed it into law on October 22, he described it as "the most comprehensive gun control law ever signed in this nation's history" (Johnson 1968b). The new law updated and expanded the National Firearms Act to cover such destructive devices as bombs, land mines, and hand grenades. The law also repealed and replaced the Federal Firearms Act. One provision of the Gun Control Act banned the importation of military-surplus weapons and guns that were not certified for sporting uses. Another provision made certain classes of citizens ineligible to purchase guns, including minors, convicted felons, drug addicts, and people with mental health issues. The law also required all guns manufactured or sold in the United States to have serial numbers. Finally, the law prohibited interstate sales of guns and ammunition through mail order.

Congressional allies of the NRA managed to remove the provisions that would have required licenses for gun ownership and registration of guns. In his signing statement, Johnson said that these changes meant the bill "falls short" of meeting his goals. "If guns are to be kept out of the hands of the criminal, out of the hands of the insane, and out of the hands of the irresponsible, then we just must have licensing. If the criminal with a gun is to be tracked down quickly, then we must have registration in this country," he declared. "The voices that blocked these safeguards were not the voices of an aroused nation. They were the voices of a powerful lobby, a gun lobby, that has prevailed for the moment in an election year" (Johnson 1968b). Although gun control advocates in Congress introduced several measures intended to address the shortcomings, Johnson proved unable to usher them through to passage.

In the heated debate over the Gun Control Act, neither side claimed a clear victory. One outcome of the controversy surrounding its passage was hardening the partisan divide over the gun issue. Following Johnson's lead, the Democratic Party adopted platforms favoring federal gun control measures, while the Republican Party adopted platforms opposing federal control and supporting private gun ownership. While the Emergency Committee for Gun Control dissolved, the NRA expanded its membership and influence in the years following the law's passage. In 1986 the organization achieved the passage of the Firearms Owners Protection Act, which weakened some of the 1968 law's provisions. In the meantime, the U.S. Supreme Court weighed in on the constitutionality of the Gun Control Act in *Lewis v. United States* (1980). The majority held that the provision banning felons from owning guns did not violate the Second Amendment.

Further Reading

Achenbach, Joel, Scott Higham, and Sari Horwitz. 2013. "How NRA's True Believers Converted a Marksmanship Group into a Mighty Gun Lobby." *Washington Post,* January 12, 2013. https://www.washingtonpost.com

/politics/how-nras-true-believers-converted-a-marksmanship-group -into-a-mighty-gun-lobby/2013/01/12/51c62288–59b9–11e2–88d0 -c4cf65c3ad15_story.html?utm_term=.554a08952ea6.

Johnson, Lyndon B. 1968a. "The People's Right to Protection." Special Message to the Congress, June 24, 1968. *Public Papers of the Presidents, 1968–1969.* Washington, DC: U.S. Government Printing Office, 1970. https://archive .org/stream/4731573.1968.001.umich.edu/4731573.1968.001.umich .edu_djvu.txt.

Johnson, Lyndon B. 1968b. "Remarks upon Signing the Gun Control Act of 1968: October 22, 1968." The American Presidency Project. http://www.presi dency.ucsb.edu/ws/?pid=29197.

Sokol, Jason. 2018. "America Passed Gun Control in 1968. Can It Happen Again?" *New York Times,* March 22, 2018. https://www.nytimes.com /2018/03/22/opinion/gun-control-1968.html.

Spitzer, Robert J. 1995. *The Politics of Gun Control.* Chatham, NJ: Chatham House Publishers.

Westcott, Gabrielle. 2016. "The Fight for the Gun Control Act of 1968." Archives and Special Collections Blog, University of Connecticut Libraries, September 15, 2016. https://blogs.lib.uconn.edu/archives/2016/09/15/the-fight-for -the-gun-control-act-of-1968/.

Zimring, Franklin E. 1975. "Firearms and Federal Law: The Gun Control Act of 1968." *Journal of Legal Studies* 4, no. 133 (January 1, 1975). https://scholar ship.law.berkeley.edu/cgi/viewcontent.cgi?article=2114&context=facpubs.

The NRA Cincinnati Revolt (1977)

In the twenty-first century, the National Rifle Association (NRA) is widely viewed as one of the most powerful political lobbying organizations in the United States. For much of its first century in existence, however, the NRA was primarily a sportsmen's club focused on teaching marksmanship skills, sponsoring shooting competitions, and promoting hunting and conservation. Union Army officers founded the organization shortly after the American Civil War (1861–1865), feeling a patriotic duty to develop safe and responsible gun ownership practices among future generations of Americans. The NRA's shift into politics began during the 1960s, when Congress responded to a wave of urban riots and assassinations of public figures by passing the Gun Control Act of 1968. Although the NRA opposed the legislation and organized a letter-writing campaign against it, NRA executive vice president Franklin Orth responded to its passage by reassuring members that "the measure as a whole appears to be one that the sportsmen of America can live with" (Achenbach, Higham, and Horwitz 2013).

Gun control advocates maintained their forward momentum into the 1970s. In 1972, the Bureau of Alcohol, Tobacco, Firearms, and Explosives (ATF) emerged as an independent federal agency responsible for enforcing the Gun Control Act and other firearms regulations. In 1976, a federal circuit court in California ruled in *United States v. Warin* that the Second Amendment did not give private citizens the right to keep and bear arms. Many observers interpreted the decision as opening the door to stricter federal gun control regulations. "There can be no question that an organized society which fails to regulate the importation, manufacture, and transfer of highly sophisticated lethal weapons in existence today does so at its peril," the judges declared (DeConde 2001, 204). Later that year, the District of Columbia enacted a law prohibiting residents from acquiring handguns and requiring all firearms in the city to be kept unloaded and disassembled. Proponents touted the law, which ranked among the strictest gun control measures in the nation, as a contributing factor in a significant drop in gun-related homicides and suicides.

Some gun rights supporters expressed concern that these developments might lead to further limitations on gun ownership or even the confiscation of guns from private citizens. Factions emerged within the NRA as leaders debated whether the organization should maintain its traditional focus as a sportsmen's group or shift its emphasis toward lobbying in defense of gun rights. In 1975, the NRA established a lobbying arm called the Institute for Legislative Action (ILA). Rather than funding the ILA's lobbying efforts, however, the board of directors decided to spend $30 million to build the National Outdoor Center, a facility dedicated to recreation and conservation in New Mexico. They also signaled a withdrawal from politics by voting to move the NRA headquarters from the nation's capital to Colorado. "You had a bunch of people who wanted to turn the NRA into a sports publishing organization and get rid of guns," recalled John D. Aquilino, who worked for the ILA at that time (Achenbach, Higham, and Horwitz 2013).

A Changing of the Guard

The conflict between the two factions came to a head at the NRA annual convention in Cincinnati, Ohio, on May 21, 1977. NRA executive vice president Maxwell Rich, who took over for Orth in 1970, and other leaders sat on a dais at the front of the hall to address the 30,000 members in attendance. Their moderate platform soon faced a vocal challenge from a grassroots group of hard-liners led by Harlon B. Carter, the founding director of the ILA, and Neal Knox, a gun magazine editor and Second Amendment activist. The hard-liners argued that the NRA needed to adjust its strategy to adapt to changing times. They viewed the passage of the Gun Control Act as an attempt by the government to deprive law-abiding citizens of their gun ownership rights. "Gun prohibition is the inevitable harbinger of oppression," Carter warned. "Without a single exception in the history of all peoples, those who are oppressed never—repeat, never—have arms" (DeConde 2001, 211). The activists demanded that the NRA stand up and fight in the political arena to eliminate gun restrictions and block future gun control legislation.

Knox presented a list of 15 demands to the NRA board of directors. When the organization's leaders refused to meet the demands, the rebels took advantage of a provision in the NRA bylaws that gave members the power to change the organization's governing structure through a vote on the convention floor. Wearing blaze-orange hunting caps and communicating with walkie-talkies, the grassroots organizers worked the room for hours to garner support for their position. Carter—a former border patrol agent and target-shooting national champion—criticized NRA leaders for wavering in their defense of gun rights and promised to take an uncompromising approach. "We can win it on a simple concept—*No compromise. No gun legislation*," he declared (Achenbach, Higham, and Horwitz 2013).

The tense debate continued into the early morning hours of May 22. The convention hall grew unbearably hot, and members consumed all of the soda in the vending machines. Rumors circulated that NRA leaders had turned off the air-conditioning in an attempt to discourage the dissidents. Finally, around 3:00 a.m. the members in attendance voted to oust Rich and other top officials and install Carter as the new head of the organization. "There will be no more civil war within the National Rifle Association," Carter declared. "It ended the hour I took office" (Suess 2018). He immediately announced that the NRA headquarters would remain in Washington, D.C., because "this is where the action is" (Achenbach, Higham, and Horwitz 2013). Knox became the new director of the ILA.

A Shift in Strategy

The historic 1977 overthrow of the NRA's leadership has become known as the Cincinnati Revolt. It led to a shift in the organization's core purpose and strategic direction that has persisted over the decades since. "What unfolded that hot night in Cincinnati forever reoriented the NRA. And this was an event with broader national reverberations," according to the *Washington Post.* "The NRA overcame tremendous internal tumult and existential crises, developed an astonishing grass-roots operation, and became closely aligned with the Republican Party. Today it is arguably the most powerful lobbying organization in the nation's capital and certainly one of the most feared" (Achenbach, Higham, and Horwitz 2013).

Carter and his followers promoted an absolutist interpretation of the Second Amendment, arguing that it granted U.S. citizens a fundamental right to own and use guns without government intrusion. They portrayed any proposed gun control measures as attempts to disarm law-abiding citizens, deny their constitutional rights to own guns for protection and pleasure, and threaten their freedom. The change in the NRA's direction appealed to many gun owners, and membership more than tripled from 1.2 million in the 1970s to over 4 million in the twenty-first century.

Under the new leadership, the NRA became a single-issue organization focused on rolling back existing gun control laws and preventing the passage of new legislation. NRA leaders built a large and highly effective lobbying organization that wielded tremendous influence in Washington, D.C., as well as in statehouses across the country. In 1986, NRA lobbyists succeeded in convincing Congress to pass the Firearm Owners Protection Act, which weakened some of the provisions of the Gun Control Act and prohibited the federal government from creating a national database of gun ownership.

In the twenty-first century, a series of mass shootings at schools and colleges in the United States prompted renewed public calls for federal gun control legislation. Following each mass shooting, new organizations formed, movements arose, and activists emerged to demand that Congress take action to restrict access to assault weapons, high-capacity magazines, and other firearms and equipment commonly used in such attacks. In each case, the NRA mobilized its members to fight against the proposed legislation. Although some NRA leaders came under criticism for making controversial statements in the aftermath of school shootings, the resulting media attention often led to an increase in membership. Following the 2012 shooting at Sandy Hook Elementary School in Newtown, Connecticut, in which 20 first-grade students and 6 staff members were killed, the NRA reportedly gained 100,000 new members.

Further Reading

Achenbach, Joel, Scott Higham, and Sari Horwitz. 2013. "How NRA's True Believers Converted a Marksmanship Group into a Mighty Gun Lobby." *Washington Post,* January 12, 2013. https://www.washingtonpost.com

/politics/how-nras-true-believers-converted-a-marksmanship-group-into
-a-mighty-gun-lobby/2013/01/12/51c62288-59b9-11e2-88d0-c4cf65
c3ad15_story.html?utm_term=.554a08952ea6.

DeConde, Alexander. 2001. *Gun Violence in America: The Struggle for Control.*
Boston: Northeastern University Press.

Stuart, Reginald. 1977. "Rifle Group Ousts Most Leaders in Move to Bolster
Stand on Guns." *New York Times,* May 23, 1977. https://www.nytimes
.com/1977/05/23/archives/rifle-group-ousts-most-leaders-in-move-to
-bolster-stand-on-guns.html.

Suess, Jeff. 2018. "NRA: 'Revolt at Cincinnati' Molded National Rifle Association." *Cincinnati Enquirer,* March 8, 2018. https://www.cincinnati.com
/story/news/politics/2018/03/08/revolt-cincinnati-molded-nra-did-you
-know-jeff-suess-schism-within-national-rifle-association-led/4046
28002/.

The Firearms Owners' Protection Act (1986)

In many ways, the modern National Rifle Association (NRA) grew out
of the passage of the Gun Control Act of 1968, which placed restrictions
on interstate gun sales and gave the Bureau of Alcohol, Tobacco, Firearms
and Explosives (ATF) power to enforce them. During the 1970s, the
impact of this legislation spurred NRA leaders to shift the organization's
focus from promoting sport shooting to defending gun rights. By the
1980s, the NRA had grown into an effective lobbying force that wielded
significant influence in Washington, D.C. The top priorities for NRA lobbyists during this era included repealing various provisions of the Gun
Control Act and curtailing the activities of the ATF.

The ATF earned the wrath of the NRA by using its authority to crack
down on gun dealers who failed to obey federal law. Under the Gun Control Act, individuals and businesses involved in manufacturing, import-
ing, or selling firearms were required to hold Federal Firearms Licenses
(FFLs). ATF agents enforced federal regulations by conducting inspections and reviewing records of gun dealers. Those found to have violated
the law by selling firearms to prohibited groups (such as minors, convicted felons, and people with drug addiction or mental illness) or illegally across state lines could be held legally liable and face revocation of
their FFLs.

Some gun dealers claimed that ATF inspectors abused their enforcement power to harass them and drive them out of business. NRA lobbyists argued that ATF agents used little-known or confusing provisions of
the Gun Control Act to entrap gun sellers, creating a situation in which

"even an honest, accidental violation was a felony" (Hardy 2011). At the behest of the NRA, the U.S. Senate formed a subcommittee to investigate gun rights. In February 1982, the subcommittee issued a report calling for reform of federal gun control laws to "enhance vital protection of constitutional and civil liberties of those Americans who choose to exercise their Second Amendment right to keep and bear arms." The report concluded that "enforcement tactics made possible by current federal firearms laws are constitutionally, legally, and practically reprehensible" (U.S. Senate 1982).

FOPA Provisions Favor Gun Owners

On the strength of the Senate subcommittee report, NRA lobbyists increased their efforts to convince gun rights supporters in Congress to pass a new law eliminating restrictions on gun sales and reining in ATF enforcement powers. After years of pressure and negotiations, they finally achieved passage of the Firearms Owners' Protection Act (FOPA), which President Ronald Reagan signed into law on May 19, 1986. FOPA significantly revised and weakened the Gun Control Act. Analysts proclaimed most provisions of the new law to be highly favorable to gun rights supporters, and NRA officials celebrated it as "the law that saved gun rights." "The fight seemed impossible, yet we won," wrote Dave Hardy of the NRA's Institute for Legislative Action (ILA). "FOPA, as it became known, didn't just change the restrictive Gun Control Act of 1968, it overruled no fewer than six anti-gun Supreme Court decisions and about one-third of the hundreds of lower court rulings interpreting the Gun Control Act" (Hardy 2011).

FOPA included many provisions aimed at loosening federal restrictions on gun sales. It legalized mail-order shipments of ammunition, removed record-keeping requirements for most ammunition sales, allowed for limited interstate sales of long guns (such as rifles and shotguns), and permitted licensed dealers to sell firearms at gun shows. FOPA also reduced enforcement of federal gun laws by limiting ATF inspections of gun dealers to once per year, narrowing the definition of "gun dealer" so that fewer private sellers would require FFLs, and prohibiting the government from compiling a national registry of gun ownership from dealer records. The law also curtailed ATF activities by raising the burden of proof for prosecutions of illegal gun sales to require violations to be intentional and willful. Finally, FOPA granted federal protection to gun owners who transported firearms across state lines. As long as travelers were only passing through a jurisdiction with strict gun control laws, they could legally possess firearms that would otherwise be illegal as long as the weapons were unloaded, not readily accessible, and locked in a separate container or compartment in the vehicle.

Gun Control Amendment Generates Controversy

Although most provisions of FOPA pleased gun rights supporters, gun control advocates scored a victory with the legislation as well. During the final stages of debate over the bill in the U.S. House of Representatives, New Jersey Democrat William J. Hughes introduced Amendment 777. It inserted a provision banning civilian sales, purchases, or ownership of automatic weapons—defined as guns that fire continuously, such as machine guns—produced after the date of the bill's passage. Although it did not affect machine guns already in private hands, the amendment ensured that all newly manufactured machine guns would be restricted to military and law enforcement personnel.

Although NRA leaders objected to the measure, they ultimately accepted it as a necessary condition to secure passage of FOPA. "The Hughes amendment created a dilemma," Hardy acknowledged. "Many House members were already being attacked as tools of the demonic 'gun lobby,' and already feared they had stuck their necks out too far. To rouse them on behalf of fully automatic firearms was hopeless. The amendment could not be removed. The choice was to accept the bill as a package, or to kill it as a package" (Hardy 2011). NRA lobbyists thus offered little resistance as the machine-gun ban passed the House on a voice vote and formally became part of FOPA.

Automatic weapons had been subject to federal restrictions since 1934, when the National Firearms Act imposed a tax on them and established a national ownership registry. This law led to a steep decline in machine-gun sales and ownership. As a result, according to gun law expert Robert Spitzer, "when the provision was added to the Firearms Owners' Protection Act to bar any newly produced fully automatic weapon from possession by civilians, it was really a fairly small step to make, because so few of them were in circulation to begin with" (Welna 2013). To obtain one of the few machine guns available to civilians, FOPA required prospective buyers to obtain an ATF license, pass a federal background check, pay a tax, and designate a licensed dealer to take legal possession of the weapon upon the owner's death. The limited supply of machine guns also caused an escalation in the average price to more than $10,000.

Some NRA members expressed outrage at the organization's acceptance of the automatic weapons restrictions, arguing that the controversial amendment threatened their Second Amendment rights. "As we learned immediately, an element of NRA, a very vociferous element of NRA . . . determined that it just couldn't be that way," said Warren Cassidy, who served as head of the ILA at that time. "We couldn't give an inch. I don't think they ever forgave me for it" (Welna 2013). Observers on both sides of the gun debate came to view FOPA's machine-gun ban as a precedent that had the potential to lead to restrictions on civilian access to other military-style firearms, such as semiautomatic assault weapons.

In general, though, historians consider the passage of FOPA to be a key moment for the gun rights movement, when the NRA proved that it had the power to push for favorable legislation rather than merely block gun control measures. "They've had other successes, but nothing in one stroke that was as significant as this," Spitzer stated (Yablon 2018). FOPA made it much more difficult for ATF agents to uncover illegal gun sales and prosecute unlicensed firearms dealers. In fact, due to FOPA limits, only around 4,000 of the 60,000 licensed gun dealers in the United States are subject to ATF inspections each year (Yablon 2018). According to Spitzer, the NRA and other gun rights supporters have been "extremely successful at demonizing, belittling and hemming in the ATF as a government regulatory agency" (Berlow 2013).

Further Reading

Berlow, Alan. 2013. "How the NRA Hobbled the ATF." *Mother Jones*, February 11, 2013. https://www.motherjones.com/politics/2013/02/atf-gun-laws-nra/.

Bixby, Scott. 2015. "Thirty Years after Banning the Sale of Machine Guns, Here's How Easy It Is to Get One." Mic, October 19, 2015. https://mic.com/articles/126943/30-years-after-banning-the-sale-of-machine-guns-here-s-how-easy-it-is-to-buy-one#.TIvQfwfpN.

Hardy, Dave. 2011. "No Surrender: The Firearms Owners' Protection Act (FOPA)." NRA-ILA, January 25, 2011. https://www.nraila.org/articles/20110125/no-surrender.

U.S. Senate. 1982. *The Right to Keep and Bear Arms: Report of the Subcommittee on the Constitution of the Committee on the Judiciary, United States Senate, Ninety-Seventh Congress, Second Session*. Washington, DC: U.S. Government Printing Office.

Welna, David. 2013. "The Decades-Old Gun Ban That's Still on the Books." National Public Radio, January 16, 2013. https://www.npr.org/sections/itsallpolitics/2013/01/18/169526687/the-decades-old-gun-ban-thats-still-on-the-books.

Yablon, Alex. 2018. "How 'The Law That Saved Gun Rights' Gutted ATF Oversight of Firearm Dealers." The Trace, June 7, 2018. https://www.thetrace.org/rounds/firearm-owners-protection-act-atf-gun-dealers/.

The Brady Bill and Assault Weapons Ban (1993–1994)

Passage of the Firearms Owners' Protection Act (FOPA) of 1986 ignited a new round of contentious debate between gun rights supporters and gun control advocates. The law loosened restrictions on gun sales that had been put in place under the Gun Control Act of 1968 and curtailed the enforcement power of the Bureau of Alcohol, Tobacco, Firearms, and Explosives (ATF). Gun control advocates expressed concern that these measures made it easier for people who were not allowed to own guns under federal law—such as convicted felons and people with mental illness—to obtain them illegally. Advocates argued that a national, computerized system of criminal background checks was needed to prevent dangerous or unstable individuals from gaining access to firearms.

In 1987, gun control advocates introduced legislation intended to address some of the problems they saw with FOPA. They called the proposed bill the Brady Handgun Violence Prevention Act in honor of James Brady, a former White House press secretary who was shot in the head and permanently disabled during a 1981 assassination attempt on President Ronald Reagan. A man with a history of mental illness, John Hinckley Jr., fired a gun he purchased at a pawn shop at the president and members of his cabinet as they exited a hotel in Washington, D.C. Reagan and two law enforcement officers were wounded in the attack, but they all recovered from their injuries. Brady sustained a severe head injury that caused him to experience cognitive issues, speech difficulties, and partial paralysis for the rest of his life.

Following the shooting, Brady's wife, Sarah Brady, emerged as a prominent gun control advocate. She served as chair of the sister organizations Handgun Control Inc. and the Center to Prevent Handgun Violence, which were eventually renamed the Brady Campaign to Prevent Gun Violence and the Brady Center to Prevent Gun Violence. Sarah Brady led the campaign to require mandatory background checks for gun purchases, which she claimed could have prevented Hinckley from acquiring the weapon he used to shoot her husband. Although the National Rifle Association (NRA) and other gun rights groups managed to defeat the Brady Bill when it was introduced in 1987 and 1991, Congress finally passed the measure in 1993. President Bill Clinton signed it into law on November 30, and it took effect three months later.

Provisions of the Brady Bill

The main provision of the Brady Bill required licensed gun dealers, manufacturers, and importers to conduct background checks on individual firearm purchasers. It also authorized creation of the National Instant Criminal Background Check System (NICS), maintained by the Federal Bureau of Investigation (FBI), to enable these checks to be completed quickly and accurately. Until the FBI developed a computerized NICS database in 1998, the Brady Bill mandated a five-day waiting period for handgun sales to facilitate the completion of background checks. The purpose of background checks was to prevent the purchase of guns by individuals who were prohibited from owning them under federal law, including convicted felons, fugitives from justice, domestic abusers, people dishonorably discharged from the military, people residing in the United States unlawfully, and people with documented drug addiction or mental illness.

The Brady Bill did not apply to unlicensed private sellers who were not engaged in firearms dealing as a business, although some state and local laws required background checks for such transactions. The Brady Bill also allowed some exceptions to mandatory NICS checks for individuals who offered proof of a previous federal background check or held a state-issued concealed carry permit. Because FOPA prohibited the federal government from compiling a national registry of gun ownership, firearms dealers could receive information about individual purchasers from the NICS database but could not submit information to the FBI about gun purchases. The NRA launched legal challenges to the Brady Bill in several states, arguing that the law was unconstitutional because it compelled state and local law enforcement officers to perform background checks. Although the U.S. Supreme Court struck down that provision in *Printz v. United States* (1997), it upheld the rest of the statute, and most jurisdictions continued to perform background checks on a voluntary basis.

According to the Brady Campaign, the law resulted in the denial of more than 2.1 million gun purchases from 1994 through 2014, or about 343 purchase attempts per day. Around 70 percent of blocked sales occurred because mandatory background checks revealed that the purchaser was a felon, a fugitive, or a domestic abuser (Fuson 2014). Former ATF director John Magaw called the Brady Bill "a historic and strong piece of legislation" and "the most important factor in keeping guns away from the people who shouldn't have them" (Johnson 2014). Gun rights supporters, on the other hand, argued that background checks were intrusive and ineffective in reducing gun violence. In response, gun control advocates pointed out that up to 40 percent of gun sales were not subject to Brady background checks, including those made online and at gun shows by unlicensed private sellers. In 2013, following a mass shooting at Sandy Hook Elementary School in Newtown, Connecticut, members of Congress introduced new legislation intended to close this loophole and require universal background checks on all commercial gun sales, but their attempt to expand the Brady Bill failed to pass.

The Federal Assault Weapons Ban

On September 13, 1994—less than a year after Congress passed the Brady Bill—President Bill Clinton signed another significant gun control measure into law. The Public Safety and Recreational Firearms Use Protection Act, commonly known as the federal assault weapons ban, passed as part of sweeping legislation called the Violent Crime Control and Law Enforcement Act. The controversial provision instituted a 10-year federal ban on the manufacture, sale, or possession of firearms defined as semiautomatic assault weapons. The list of prohibited weapons included 19 specific military-style models—such as the AR-15, AK-47, and Uzi— as well as other semiautomatic firearms with detachable magazines and certain other features, including pistol grips, folding or telescoping stocks, and flash suppressors. The law also banned the sale of high-capacity ammunition magazines, which it defined as capable of firing more than 10 rounds in succession. It did not apply to the estimated 1 million assault weapons already in the legal possession of private citizens at the time the ban took effect, and it featured a sunset provision that meant the ban expired after 10 years.

Public support for an assault weapons ban grew in the wake of several mass shootings in which the perpetrators used semiautomatic firearms, including a 1989 incident in which a gunman armed with an AK-47 shot 34 children and one teacher at Cleveland Elementary School in Stockton, California. When Senator Dianne Feinstein, a Democrat from California, first proposed the federal assault weapons ban in 1993, polls indicated that more than three-quarters of Americans favored the measure (Eaton 1994). Former presidents Gerald Ford, Jimmy Carter, and Ronald Reagan all signed a letter asking Congress to pass the legislation, calling it "a matter of vital importance to the public safety" (Eaton 1994). The NRA and other gun rights supporters opposed the ban, arguing that it unfairly targeted a category of weapons that were used in an insignificant percentage of crimes. Although they could not prevent passage of the bill, NRA lobbyists and their allies in Congress did manage to weaken it and add the sunset provision.

The federal assault weapons ban expired on September 13, 2004. Although Feinstein and other members of Congress have proposed numerous bills to renew or expand the ban—including after the Sandy Hook school shooting in 2012—their efforts have proven unsuccessful. For some gun control advocates, however, banning assault weapons did not rank among their top priorities. Critics contend that the 1994–2004 ban focused on cosmetic features of semiautomatic weapons, which made it easy for gun manufacturers to circumvent the law by making slight design changes to prohibited firearms. Instead, some gun control groups shifted their attention toward banning large-capacity magazines (LCMs), which are what make assault weapons so devastating in mass shooting situations. They pointed to research suggesting that LCMs were used in 14 to 25 percent of all gun crimes, whereas assault weapons were only used in 2 to 8 percent (Seitz-Wald 2013).

Further Reading

Eaton, William. 1994. "Ford, Carter, Reagan Push for Gun Ban." *Los Angeles Times,* May 5, 1994. http://articles.latimes.com/1994-05-05/news/mn-54185_1 _assault-weapons-ban/2.

Fuson, Jennifer. 2014. "Brady Campaign Releases a Report Analyzing 20 Years of Effective Background Checks." Brady Campaign, February 28, 2014. http://www.bradycampaign.org/inthenews/brady-campaign-releases -a-report-analyzing-20-years-of-effective-background-checks.

Johnson, Kevin. 2014. "Brady Had Lasting Impact on Gun Control." *USA Today,* August 4, 2014. https://www.usatoday.com/story/news/politics/2014/08 /04/brady-campaign-gun-control/13583365/.

Kurtzleben, Danielle. 2016. "Research Suggests Gun Background Checks Work, but They're Not Everything." National Public Radio, January 9, 2016. https://www.npr.org/2016/01/09/462252799/research-suggests-gun -background-checks-work-but-theyre-not-everything.

Seitz-Wald, Alex. 2013. "Don't Mourn the Assault Weapons Ban's Impending Demise." Salon, February 6, 2013. https://www.salon.com/2013/02/06 /dont_mourn_the_assault_weapons_bans_impending_demise/.

The Columbine High School Shooting (1999)

The first U.S. school shooting to receive round-the-clock media attention occurred on April 20, 1999, at Columbine High School near Littleton, Colorado. Two students armed with guns and explosive devices waged a 49-minute attack in which they killed 12 fellow students and 1 educator and injured two dozen other people. At the time, it was the deadliest school shooting on record and the fifth-deadliest mass shooting in the United States since World War II. Millions of Americans viewed footage of the shooting and its aftermath on television news channels or on the Internet.

As one of the first events of its magnitude, Columbine generated a profound sense of shock and disillusionment. It raised questions, prompted reassessments, and initiated changes to policies involving mental health care, school safety, police tactics, and media coverage. "What is indisputable is that Columbine quickly became a byword for the nightmarish phenomenon—now seemingly a worldwide contagion—of school shootings," Andrew Gumbel wrote in *The Guardian*. "It was the bloodiest, creepiest, most vivid school attack anyone at the time could remember and remains, to this day, the episode the American popular imagination just can't seem to shake" (Gumbel 2009).

The Incident

The perpetrators of the attack on Columbine High School, seniors Eric Harris and Dylan Klebold, planned it meticulously for months beforehand. They acquired two 12-gauge shotguns, a 9mm carbine, and a 9mm semiautomatic handgun. Since they were too young to purchase guns legally, they completed the transactions through friends as illegal straw purchases. They also downloaded instructions from the Internet and built 99 makeshift explosive devices, ranging from small carbon dioxide canister bombs to 20-pound propane tank bombs. Throughout this process, they recorded their violent impulses in personal journals and online blogs and documented their preparations in a series of home videos.

Inspired by the Oklahoma City bombing, which destroyed a federal office building and killed 168 people on April 19, 1995, the perpetrators originally intended to carry out a terrorist bombing at Columbine. They arrived at the school separately at 11:10 a.m., parked in lots on opposite sides of the building, and set the bombs concealed inside their vehicles to detonate at noon. Since the attack would be under way at that time, the car bombs were meant to kill or injure fleeing survivors, emergency responders, and reporters. The perpetrators then made their way to the school cafeteria, where they planted two propane bombs hidden inside duffel bags, set them to detonate at 11:17, and went back outside to wait. If these devices had exploded as planned, they could have killed or seriously injured the 500 students who were just arriving for lunch and possibly collapsed the floor of the library above. When the bombs failed to detonate, the perpetrators approached the building at 11:19, pulled guns from beneath dark trench coats, and began shooting people.

By 11:22, school resource officer Neil Gardner received an emergency call about the shooters and drove around the building toward the cafeteria. Three minutes later he engaged in a shootout with Harris from his position in the school parking lot, but no one was hit. A few minutes later, two Jefferson County Sheriff Department deputies arrived on the scene. They also exchanged shots with Harris before beginning to help frightened and injured students who were fleeing from the building. Meanwhile, Columbine physical education teacher Dave Sanders worked to evacuate students from the cafeteria. After escorting groups of students to safety in locked classrooms, Sanders encountered the perpetrators in a hallway and was mortally wounded. Fellow teachers helped him into a science classroom, where students trained in first aid provided emergency treatment, called 911, and waited for paramedics to arrive.

At 11:29, the shooters entered the library, where 52 students and 4 faculty members hid beneath desks or behind bookshelves. Art teacher Patti Nielson had already called 911 and remained on the phone with an emergency operator when the perpetrators came in. They walked casually around the room, often laughing, howling, and taunting fellow students by asking if they believed in God or if they wanted to die. They killed 10 people and wounded 12 others before leaving the library at 11:35. For the next half hour the perpetrators wandered through the halls of the school, lobbing pipe bombs and shooting at random targets. At one point, they returned to the cafeteria and tried unsuccessfully to ignite the propane bombs. Finally, at 12:08—49 minutes after the shooting began—the perpetrators committed suicide.

The Aftermath

The Columbine massacre dominated the national news for weeks, as the American people struggled to understand why it happened and how it could have been prevented. In attempting to answer these questions, the feverish media coverage perpetuated many myths about the perpetrators and their motives. Many reports portrayed the gunmen as social outcasts and victims of bullying, for instance, and attributed their actions to a desire to exact revenge against popular jocks who tormented them. Other reports claimed that the perpetrators belonged to a shadowy campus group known as the Trenchcoat Mafia and were influenced by goth subculture or the music of Marilyn Manson. Various reports attributed the attack to the perpetrators' interest in violent video games or use of antidepressant medications. Later investigations showed, however, that "all those stories were the product of hysteria, ignorance, and flailing guesswork in the first few hours and days" (Gumbel 2009). Yet even though the narratives proved to be false, they entered the public consciousness and impacted the way people thought about mass shooters from that time forward.

After examining the perpetrators' journals and interviewing people who knew them, psychiatrists determined that both Harris and Klebold had mental health issues that probably contributed to their actions. Harris exhibited many signs of psychopathy, including self-aggrandizement, deceitfulness, callousness, contempt for others, and a lack of conscience, empathy, or remorse. Klebold struggled with depression, suicidal ideation, intense anger, and an uncontrollable temper. "Klebold was hurting inside while Harris wanted to hurt people," said Dwayne Fuselier, lead Columbine investigator for the Federal Bureau of Investigation (FBI). Their plan to blow up the high school grew out of a generalized hatred of other people combined with an intense desire for notoriety. Rather than targeting specific individuals, experts claim, they picked a familiar target that would allow them to kill as many people as possible.

Investigations showed that the perpetrators signaled their violent intentions in many ways, yet authorities failed to recognize or act on the information. Harris made violent threats against Columbine teachers and students on a publicly accessible website, for instance, which a classmate's parents brought to the attention of the Jefferson County Sheriff's Office. Although deputies found the threats credible enough to apply for a warrant to search Harris's home, they never executed the search warrant and concealed their prior knowledge of his threatening behavior from the media. Two months before the attack, Klebold wrote an essay for English class describing a mass shooting in graphic detail from the gunman's perspective. Although his teacher expressed concerns, school officials ultimately believed his explanation that it was merely an imaginary exercise.

A U.S. government study of 37 school shootings that occurred between 1974 and 2000 dispelled the myth that perpetrators tended to be social misfits from broken homes. Although all of the shooters were male, they had little else in common ethnically, socially, or economically. Ninety-three percent of the perpetrators planned their attacks in advance, however, and 81 percent revealed their plans to someone (Cullen 2009b). After Columbine, students, parents, school officials, and police began to take such threats more seriously, and in some cases such vigilance prevented potential tragedies from occurring. Many school districts implemented zero-tolerance policies that required automatic suspension or expulsion for students who brought weapons to school or engaged in threatening behavior. Experts pointed out, however, that imposing such severe penalties could have the unintended consequence of making students less willing to come forward with suspicions or tips about their classmates.

The Columbine massacre led to the adoption of many other measures designed to enhance school security. Many schools installed metal detectors at entrance doors, hired armed security guards or resource officers, and required students to carry photo identification cards, wear school uniforms, or use backpacks made of transparent material. Other districts worked to improve public safety by numbering school doors, providing authorities with up-to-date floor plans, and implementing lockdown drills and evacuation plans.

Some of the most significant post-Columbine changes came in the area of law enforcement response. Critics pointed out that the school resource officer assigned to Columbine High School arrived within five minutes after the shooting began, and half a dozen local police officers responded a few minutes later. Despite gathering information from multiple 911 calls and from escaping students, however, no law enforcement personnel entered the building for 47 minutes. Instead, they established a perimeter and waited for SWAT teams to assemble. Friends and family members of victims asserted that a quicker, more aggressive police response could have saved lives. "There seemed like there was a lot of officers walking around outside with nothing to do," said student survivor Melanie Poleshook, who waited in a classroom with wounded teacher Dave Sanders for nearly three hours. By the time help finally arrived, Sanders had bled to death. "I don't know why they couldn't have sent maybe a few more people directly to come to our room," she stated (Kohn 2001).

Law enforcement officials defended their decisions during the Columbine shooting, arguing that they followed accepted procedure at that time. They also noted several factors that complicated the response, including questions about the number of shooters, concerns about encountering bombs or booby traps, and confusion caused by smoke, sprinklers, blaring fire alarms, and fleeing students. "They believed that they really had six to eight armed individuals inside there," said SWAT team trainer Larry Glick. "And if you're in those shoes of those officers, they felt that it was more reasonable to wait until additional personnel responded to move in" (Kohn 2001). In the wake of Columbine, police departments across the country reassessed their training programs and devised a new type of tactical response called an active-shooter protocol. Since the goal of mass shooters is to kill as many people as quickly as possible, the new strategy for law enforcement emphasized entering the building immediately, moving toward the sounds of gunfire, and stopping the shooter by whatever means necessary.

The media frenzy that surrounded the Columbine massacre also generated criticism and prompted changes to press coverage of future incidents. The rush to uncover information led to sensational and irresponsible reporting by some news outlets. Critics argued that the extensive media coverage gave the perpetrators so much notoriety that it inspired other deranged attention seekers to plan copycat crimes. Since Columbine, the American news media has changed its approach by emphasizing the humanity of the victims of mass shootings and downplaying the actions of the perpetrators. In fact, some survivors of gun violence have pressured media outlets to refrain from mentioning the names of gunmen. "I think we in the media have to look at our own role in this," said journalist Dave Cullen, author of *Columbine*. "We didn't know the spark would be lit that would become this thing, these mass murders, that would go on and on and really ramp up 12 to 15 years later. We didn't know all that was going to happen. But now we do. And I think we're starting to realize we have sort of played a role. We didn't start it. But we have sure been hurling the gasoline on, or allowing it, really gassing it up. So it's different now" (Calderone 2013).

Further Reading

Calderone, Michael. 2013. "Columbine Author Dave Cullen Criticizes Media's Handling of Mass Shootings." Huffington Post, September 17, 2013. https://www.huffingtonpost.com/2013/09/17/columbine-dave-cullen -mass-shootings_n_3943713.html.

Cullen, Dave. 2004. "The Depressive and the Psychopath." Slate, April 20, 2004. http://www.slate.com/articles/news_and_politics/assessment/2004/04 /the_depressive_and_the_psychopath.html.

Cullen, Dave. 2009a. *Columbine*. New York: Twelve.

Cullen, Dave. 2009b. "The Four Most Important Lessons of Columbine." Slate, April 29, 2009. http://www.slate.com/articles/news_and_politics/history _lesson/2009/04/the_four_most_important_lessons_of_columbine .html.

Gumbel, Andrew. 2009. "The Truth about Columbine." *The Guardian*, April 16, 2009. https://www.theguardian.com/world/2009/apr/17/columbine-mass acre-gun-crime-us.

Kohn, David. 2001. "What Really Happened at Columbine?" CBS News, April 17, 2001. https://www.cbsnews.com/news/what-really-happened-at -columbine/.

The Virginia Tech Shooting (2007)

The deadliest school shooting in U.S. history took place on April 16, 2007, on the campus of Virginia Polytechnic Institute and State University (known as Virginia Tech) in Blacksburg, Virginia. A 23-year-old student armed with two semiautomatic handguns killed 27 students and 5 faculty members and injured more than a dozen other people. The perpetrator, who had a history of mental illness, left behind a deranged video manifesto in which he complained about wealthy "brats" and "snobs" at Virginia Tech and expressed admiration for the gunmen who killed 13 people at Columbine High School in Colorado in 1999.

The Virginia Tech shooting reignited the national debate about gun violence prevention. Gun control advocates pushed to strengthen federal background checks to prevent people with mental disorders from purchasing guns. Gun rights supporters pushed to eliminate rules prohibiting gun owners from carrying their weapons on college campuses, arguing that armed civilians could help stop mass shooters. After Virginia Tech administrators came under criticism for their handling of the incident, many colleges and universities introduced changes designed to increase campus safety.

The Incident

The perpetrator of the Virginia Tech shooting, Seung Hui Cho, was born in South Korea but moved to the United States in 1992 and became a permanent legal resident. He was a senior at the university and majored in English. Described as a loner who rarely spoke to anyone, Cho began showing signs of deteriorating mental health in 2005. His English professors reported him to campus police for displaying antisocial behavior in class, such as taking cell phone pictures of female students without their permission and turning in creative writing assignments filled with violent imagery and obscene themes. Following charges that Cho stalked female students and expressed suicidal thoughts to his roommates, a Virginia court declared him mentally ill in December 2005 and ordered him to undergo outpatient psychiatric treatment at a mental health care facility. He never complied with the order.

Sixteen months later, Cho entered West Ambler Johnston Hall, a coed dormitory that housed nearly 900 students, armed with two semiautomatic handguns. At around 7:15 a.m., he shot and killed a female freshman student in her room and a male resident adviser who apparently came to her aid. The gunman then left the dormitory and returned to his own nearby residence hall to change clothes. Police responding to the shooting initially treated it as a domestic violence incident and sought the female student's boyfriend as the main suspect. Because they did not anticipate any further violence, they did not issue a campus-wide emergency alert. Instead, they notified students and faculty of the shooting via e-mail at 9:26, more than two hours after it occurred.

Meanwhile, the shooter walked to a local post office. At 9:01, he mailed a package to NBC News in New York City. Then he walked across campus and at around 9:40 entered Norris Hall, a building where he once attended class, carrying the two handguns and 400 rounds of ammunition. After chaining and locking the exit doors, the perpetrator went from classroom to classroom on the second floor, methodically shooting students and faculty members. Some students tried to barricade the classroom doors, while others hid beneath desks or jumped out of windows to escape. After murdering 30 people within about 10 minutes, the gunman committed suicide. At 9:50, university officials sent a second e-mail warning students that there was an active shooter on campus and asking them to shelter in place. An hour later, Virginia Tech administrators sent another e-mail saying that the gunman was in custody.

Two days later, on April 18, NBC News received the package Cho had sent between the shootings at the dormitory and at Norris Hall. It contained photographs, written material, and an angry video in which he ranted about perceived wrongs, blamed unnamed tormentors for his violent rampage, and claimed that his actions would inspire other oppressed people. After consulting with law enforcement, NBC made the controversial decision to air portions of the material publicly. Some survivors of the shooting and families of the victims said that releasing the material added to their trauma. Other critics objected to the fact that the network provided the perpetrator with a platform for his message and validated his delusional thinking, which they worried might encourage copycat crimes. Referring to the widespread publication of the material as a "social catastrophe," forensic psychiatrist Michael Welner noted that "He did this to achieve immortality. We have to stop giving him that" (ABC News 2007).

The Aftermath

In response to the Virginia Tech massacre, gun control advocates intensified their campaign to strengthen the National Instant Criminal Background Check System (NICS) to prevent people with mental health issues from purchasing firearms. "We feel if the shooter at Virginia Tech was in this background check, he may not have been able to obtain a gun," said Barbara La Porte of the Virginia Tech Victims Family Outreach Foundation (Pelletiere 2017). Although Cho had been adjudicated as mentally ill, state law only denied firearm purchases to individuals who were institutionalized for psychiatric disorders. Since Cho had received outpatient treatment, the state of Virginia did not submit information about his mental health status to the federal database. Virginia lawmakers closed this legal loophole in the wake of the shooting. In addition, Congress passed the NICS Improvement Amendments Act, which established stricter standards for state reporting of mental health data for background checks on gun sales. President George W. Bush signed it into law on January 5, 2008.

At the same time, gun rights lobbyists argued that the key to preventing mass shootings such as the one at Virginia Tech was to allow citizens to carry guns on college campuses. "There has been this crescendo of mass shootings that have driven people to say, 'We need more lawful people who can protect themselves and stop these things,'" said Erich Pratt of the Gun Owners of America (Jervis 2017). Within a decade of the Virginia Tech shootings, the campaign resulted in 10 states passing laws to allow guns on the campuses of public universities.

In the aftermath of the shooting, Virginia Tech administrators came under criticism for their handling of the active-shooter situation on campus. Critics argued that university officials should have issued a campus-wide emergency alert and initiated a security protocol immediately after the dormitory shooting. They asserted that by sending an e-mail message two hours later, the university left students and faculty vulnerable to the second round of the attack. The Virginia Tech Review Panel, convened by Governor Tim Kaine to examine circumstances surrounding the shooting, claimed that a prompt warning could have reduced the number of casualties. In 2011, the U.S. Department of Education fined Virginia Tech for failing to meet its obligations under the Clery Act, a 1990 law related to campus crime and security. The Virginia Tech shooting prompted many colleges to review and update their security measures to include threat-assessment teams and campus-wide safety alerts.

In the spring of 2008, Virginia Tech and the State of Virginia reached a financial settlement with the families of victims of the shooting. The settlement set aside $11 million to provide $100,000 in compensation to the loved ones of each of the 32 people killed and to cover survivors' medical costs and psychiatric care. Two years after the shooting, Virginia Tech reopened Norris Hall as the site of its Center for Peace Studies and Violence Prevention.

Further Reading

ABC News. 2007. "Psychiatrist: Showing Video Is 'Social Catastrophe.'" *ABC News*, April 19, 2007. https://abcnews.go.com/GMA/VATech/story?id=3056168& page=1.

Agger, Ben, and Timothy W. Luke, eds. 2008. *There Is a Gunman on Campus: Tragedy and Terror at Virginia Tech.* Lanham, MD: Rowman and Littlefield.

Jervis, Rick. 2017. "Ten Years after Virginia Tech Shooting: How Gun Laws Have Changed." *USA Today,* April 14, 2017. https://www.usatoday.com/story /news/nation/2017/04/14/va-tech-shooting-gun-laws-debate/100458024/.

Pelletiere, Nicole. 2017. "Inside Room 211: The Massacre at Virginia Tech Remembered 10 Years Later." ABC News, April 13, 2017. https://abcnews .go.com/US/room-211-massacre-virginia-tech-remembered-10-years /story?id=46701034.

Worth, Richard. 2008. *Massacre at Virginia Tech: Disaster and Survival.* Berkeley Heights, NJ: Enslow.

District of Columbia v. Heller (2008)

In the two centuries since the U.S. Constitution was written, legal scholars, political leaders, and ordinary citizens alike have debated about the framers' intentions and the document's application to modern American society. No section of the Constitution has generated more controversy than the Second Amendment, which reads "A well regulated Militia, being necessary to the security of a free State, the right of the people to keep and bear Arms, shall not be infringed."

For many years, courts largely interpreted the Second Amendment to mean that states had the right to raise armed citizen militias to protect their sovereign interests. This interpretation protected collective gun ownership rights within the context of militia service, and the U.S. Supreme Court declined to expand gun rights beyond this context in four different rulings between 1876 and 1939. Over time, however, gun rights supporters increasingly interpreted the Second Amendment to mean that the people had a fundamental right to own guns without government interference. Under this individual rights interpretation, government efforts to regulate firearms were unconstitutional.

Some historians date the shift in interpretation of the Second Amendment to the late 1970s, when a group of hard-line gun rights activists took over leadership of the National Rifle Association (NRA) and turned it into a highly effective lobbying organization. The NRA adopted an uncompromising stance on the Second Amendment, arguing that it conveyed an absolute right for citizens to purchase firearms without restriction as well as carry them in public spaces. NRA activists portrayed any attempt to regulate firearms as a form of government tyranny and a step toward the confiscation of all guns in private hands.

NRA lobbyists succeeded in garnering support from the Republican Party, which shifted from a platform that favored restrictions on handgun sales in 1972 to a platform that opposed federal registration of firearms in 1980. The NRA also waged a campaign to influence public opinion and bring its interpretation of the Second Amendment into the mainstream. "By describing gun rights as foundational to the nation and liberty through the Second Amendment, it elevated guns and related issues into a cultural and political identity that went beyond the legal technicalities of gun control," wrote German Lopez in Vox. "That made guns feel crucial to the soul of America, and many on the right embraced the new perspective" (Lopez 2017). By 2008, when the U.S. Supreme Court considered the constitutionality of gun control laws in *District of Columbia v. Heller,* a Gallup poll showed that 73 percent of Americans believed that the Second Amendment applied to individual citizens rather than to state militias (Waldman 2014).

The Battle over Gun Rights in the District of Columbia

The Supreme Court case stemmed from a legal challenge to the Firearms Control Regulations Act of 1975, which gave the nation's capital some of the strictest gun laws in the United States when it was enacted by the District of Columbia City Council. Washington, D.C., had struggled for years with high rates of illegal drugs, crime, and gun violence. As the seat of the federal government, D.C. also faced special challenges in ensuring the safety of political leaders and foreign dignitaries. Shortly after Congress granted D.C. home rule and allowed it to establish a government in 1973, city officials strove to address these long-standing issues by banning Washington residents—other than law enforcement personnel—from owning handguns, automatic firearms, or semiautomatic weapons with high-capacity magazines. While the law made an exception for firearms lawfully owned by residents prior to 1976, it also required all guns that were kept in private homes to be unloaded, disassembled, or equipped with a trigger lock. Finally, the law established a registration system for firearms and prohibited the possession of unregistered firearms.

The D.C. handgun ban survived several attempts by Congress to overturn it and remained in place for a quarter century. In the late 1990s a group of attorneys from the libertarian Cato Institute, led by Robert Levy, began preparing a new challenge to the law. They argued that the provision requiring gun owners to keep firearms in the home unloaded or locked infringed on the Second Amendment right of law-abiding citizens to use guns for self-protection. The lead plaintiff in the case was Dick Heller, a former paratrooper who worked as an armed security guard at the Federal Judiciary Building. Since he lived in a high-crime neighborhood, Heller wanted to bring the handgun he carried at work home with him at night for self-defense. When he tried to register the weapon in 2002, D.C. officials denied his request for a permit. "I was given a gun to protect [government workers] but couldn't own a gun to protect me after I turned in my gun protecting them," Heller stated (Moyer 2018).

The case wound through the federal court system for several years before the Supreme Court agreed to hear it in 2008. In a landmark 5–4 decision issued on June 26, the court struck down key provisions of the Firearms Control Regulations Act as unconstitutional. The majority opinion, written by Justice Antonin Scalia, redefined the scope of the Second Amendment: "The Second Amendment protects an individual right to possess a firearm unconnected with service in a militia, and to use that arm for traditionally lawful purposes, such as self-defense within the home." The court ruled that D.C.'s complete ban on handgun ownership, as well as the provision requiring guns kept in the home to be unloaded or locked, violated this right.

To the relief of gun control advocates, Scalia qualified the majority decision by noting that the Second Amendment did not prohibit federal, state, or local governments from enacting reasonable restrictions on firearms. "Like most rights, the Second Amendment right is not unlimited. It is not a right to keep and carry any weapon whatsoever in any manner whatsoever and for whatever purpose," he wrote. "The Court's opinion should not be taken to cast doubt on longstanding prohibitions on the possession of firearms by felons and the mentally ill, or laws forbidding the carrying of firearms in sensitive places such as schools and government buildings, or laws imposing conditions and qualifications on the commercial sale of arms."

In his dissent, Justice John Paul Stevens argued that the decision overturned long-standing legal precedent without providing lawmakers with clear guidelines for how to proceed. "Until today, it has been understood that legislatures may regulate the civilian use and misuse of firearms so long as they do not interfere with the preservation of a well-regulated militia," he wrote. "The Court's announcement of a new constitutional right to own and use firearms for private purposes upsets that settled understanding, but leaves for future cases the formidable task of defining the scope of permissible regulations." In 2010, the Supreme Court issued a second 5–4 decision in *McDonald v. City of Chicago* that applied the *Heller* ruling to state and local governments.

The District of Columbia City Council responded to the *Heller* decision by passing new gun restrictions that stopped short of an outright handgun ban but still made it difficult for residents to obtain gun permits. When city officials denied Heller's application to register his weapon in 2008, he filed a second legal challenge against the new laws. In 2015, the Circuit Court for the District of Columbia invalidated 4 of the 10 registration requirements, including provisions that limited residents to one handgun registration per month, required them to renew gun permits every three years, and required them to pass a test on D.C. gun laws. The judges allowed 6 restrictions to stand, however, including ones that required gun owners to complete a safety class and pay a registration fee.

Impact of the Decision

People on both sides of the gun issue have debated the impact of *Washington D.C. v. Heller* throughout the decade since the Supreme Court issued its decision. Many gun rights supporters argue that it fundamentally changed the legal landscape by recognizing an individual right to gun ownership under the Second Amendment. "We live in a world where, in part because of Heller, every single American has the right to own a gun in their own home for self-defense," said constitutional law expert Adam Winkler. "His lawsuit paved the way for literally hundreds of other lawsuits. So I think his influence has really been quite huge" (Obbie 2016).

Gun control advocates, on the other hand, focus on the narrow scope of the ruling and its explicit acknowledgment that individual gun rights remained subject to government regulation. They contend that *Heller* was not as significant a victory as gun rights activists claim because it still left room for reasonable restrictions, such as background checks and prohibitions on public carry. "The courts generally strike a balance between the need for lawmakers to protect public safety and this notion of Second Amendment rights," said Avery Gardiner of the Brady Campaign to Prevent Gun Violence. "There's a mythology here that the Supreme Court has said something about the Second Amendment that it hasn't" (Yuhas 2017).

Some gun rights activists argued that the *Heller* ruling did not go far enough, because gun ownership rights remained subject to some government restriction. "As the gun-rights community has shifted right in the years since *Heller,* from strategic and pragmatic to absolutist and idealistic, the greatest casualty has been reasonable expectations," Mark Obbie wrote in a Trace article (Obbie 2016). In this way, according to gun control advocates, the Supreme Court's interpretation of the Second Amendment had a psychological and political impact that made it more difficult to pass commonsense gun laws. "The document that promises and protects our freedom has been interpreted to say that we are all condemned to live out our days in terror, hostage to powerful interests who urge us to become ever more free by purchasing and stockpiling ever more lethal weapons of war," Dahlia Lithwick wrote in a Slate article (Lithwick 2016).

Further Reading

"District of Columbia v. Heller." 2008. Oyez. https://www.oyez.org/cases/2007
/07-290.
Lithwick, Dahlia. 2016. "The Second Amendment Hoax." Slate, June 13, 2016.
http://www.slate.com/articles/news_and_politics/jurisprudence/2016/06
/how_the_nra_perverted_the_meaning_of_the_2nd_amendment.html.
Lopez, German. 2017. "How the NRA Resurrected the Second Amendment."
Vox, October 12, 2017. https://www.vox.com/policy-and-politics/2017/10
/12/16418524/nra-second-amendment-guns-violence.
Moyer, Justin W. 2018. "'The Culture's Changed': Gun Rights Supporters Mark 10
Years since Landmark Ruling Toppled D.C. Gun Ban." *Washington Post,*
June 26, 2018. https://www.washingtonpost.com/local/crime/the-cultures
-changed-gun-rights-supporters-mark-10-years-since-landmark-ruling
-toppled-dc-gun-ban/2018/06/26/02fdf738–7890–11e8-bda2
-f99f3863e603_story.html?noredirect=on&utm_term=.599d02ad0f7f.
Obbie, Mark. 2016. "He Won the Supreme Court Case That Transformed Gun
Rights. But Dick Heller Is a Hard Man to Please." The Trace, March 20,
2016. https://www.thetrace.org/2016/03/dick-heller-second-amendment
-hero-abolish-gun-regulation/.
Waldman, Michael. 2014. "How the NRA Rewrote the Second Amendment."
Politico, May 14, 2014. https://www.politico.com/magazine/story/2014
/05/nra-guns-second-amendment-106856?o=0.
Winkler, Adam. 2011. *Gunfight: The Battle over the Right to Bear Arms.* New York:
Norton.
Yuhas, Alan. 2017. "The Right to Bear Arms: What Does the Second Amendment
Really Mean?" *The Guardian,* October 5, 2017. https://www.theguardian
.com/us-news/2017/oct/05/second-amendment-right-to-bear-arms
-meaning-history.

The Sandy Hook Elementary School Shooting (2012)

On December 14, 2012, a gunman armed with an AR-15 semiautomatic rifle forced his way into Sandy Hook Elementary School in Newtown, Connecticut, and murdered 20 first-grade students and 6 educators. It was the second-deadliest school shooting in U.S. history. The unspeakable tragedy prompted President Barack Obama to propose new gun control legislation that would expand criminal background checks and reinstate a federal ban on military-style assault weapons. "As a country, we have been through this too many times," Obama declared in a tearful press briefing on what he called the worst day of his presidency. "We're going to have to come together and take meaningful action to prevent more tragedies like this, regardless of the politics" (Obama 2012). Gun rights lobbyists convinced Republicans in Congress to block the legislation, however, and instead suggested placing armed security guards in more of the nation's schools.

The Incident

Sandy Hook Elementary served around 450 students in kindergarten through fourth grade. The perpetrator of the shooting, 20-year-old Adam Lanza, attended the school as a boy. He arrived at the building around 9:30 a.m. carrying the AR-15, two semiautomatic pistols, and nearly 500 rounds of ammunition. Finding the outer security door locked, he shot out a plate glass window to gain access to the entryway. When school principal Dawn Hochsprung and school psychologist Mary Sherlach ran out of the main office to investigate, the shooter killed both women. He then shot and wounded 2 other staff members who stepped into the hallway.

Since Sandy Hook administrators had been making morning announcements when the shooter entered the building, the sounds of gunfire were broadcast over the school's public address system. Teachers and students immediately began implementing lockdown procedures, such as barricading classroom doors and concealing themselves in closets or bathrooms. The shooter burst into one first-grade classroom before it could be secured and gunned down teacher Lauren Rousseau, behavioral therapist Rachel D'Avino, and 14 students. He then entered another first-grade classroom, where teacher Victoria Soto had hidden most of her students in a closet. The gunman killed her and special education aide Ann Marie Murphy, who had wrapped her arms around a student in an attempt to protect him, as well as 6 students. When first responders arrived at Sandy Hook around 9:40, the shooter pulled out a handgun and took his own life.

After identifying the shooter, authorities went to his home and discovered that he had shot and killed his mother, Nancy Lanza, earlier that morning. She owned all of the guns used in the attack and had often visited a shooting range with her son. Investigators found no evidence that the gunman had targeted anyone specific at the school, and they uncovered no motive for the crime. They did learn that the perpetrator had been diagnosed with autism spectrum disorder during childhood and that his mental health had deteriorated significantly during his teen years, leading to social isolation. They also found evidence suggesting that the shooter developed an obsession with school shootings, including newspaper clippings and spreadsheets listing details of various incidents. In a report on the Sandy Hook massacre issued in 2013, the Connecticut state's attorney acknowledged that Lanza "had significant mental health issues that affected his ability to live a normal life and to interact with others" but also noted that "what contribution this made to the shootings, if any, is unknown as those mental health professionals who saw him did not see anything that would have predicted his future behavior" (Sedensky 2013).

The Aftermath

As the frequency of U.S. mass shootings increased in the 2000s, some Americans began to grow numb to the apparent inevitability of gun violence. Partly due to the young age of the student victims, however, the Sandy Hook shooting had a devastating emotional impact that seemed to revive public outrage. Polls taken in the weeks following the horrific events in Newtown showed a shift in public opinion about gun rights from a year earlier. The percentage of Americans who favored greater restrictions on gun ownership increased from 45 percent to 49 percent, while the percentage who felt that it was more important to protect the rights of gun owners decreased from 49 percent to 42 percent. This marked the first time in Obama's presidency that more Americans expressed support for gun control than for gun rights (Drake 2013).

Obama responded to the Sandy Hook tragedy by calling on Congress to pass meaningful new laws aimed at reducing the prevalence of mass shootings. One legislative priority involved restoring and expanding the federal ban on semiautomatic assault weapons and large-capacity ammunition magazines that had been allowed to expire in 2004. In early 2013, Democratic senator Dianne Feinstein of California proposed a bill that would have banned 150 models of firearms as well as all magazines that held more than 10 rounds of ammunition. With gun rights groups pouring $10 million into a campaign opposing it, however, the measure went down to defeat in the Senate. "In the wake of Sandy Hook, the gun rights lobby outspent, out-organized and out-maneuvered gun control advocates at both the state and federal level," according to PBS Frontline (Childress 2013).

Another legislative priority involved expanding the federal background check system to cover firearm sales conducted online or at gun shows. Despite surveys showing that 91 percent of Americans supported tighter background checks, a Republican filibuster prevented Congress from passing a proposed reform bill (Drake 2013). "An overwhelming majority of Americans felt that things like background checks . . . might save a few lives; that if a madman walks into a school intent on doing harm, fewer children might die if he doesn't have a semiautomatic weapon with magazines that can just deliver a stunning amount of bullets in a short span of time," Obama stated. "The fact that we couldn't even get something as basic as that through the Senate was heartbreaking" (Obama 2016).

Wayne LaPierre, head of the National Rifle Association (NRA), rejected the assertion that banning certain types of firearms or restricting gun sales would address the problem of school shootings. Instead, claiming that "the only way to stop a bad guy with a gun is with a good guy with a gun," he called on Congress "to appropriate whatever is necessary to put armed police officers in every single school in this nation" (Rugg and Nye 2012). LaPierre's controversial statements about the Sandy Hook shooting drew criticism from many quarters. "Instead of offering solutions to a problem they have helped create, they offered a paranoid, dystopian vision of a more dangerous and violent America where everyone is armed and no place is safe," New York mayor Michael Bloomberg said of the NRA. "Enough. As a country, we must rise above special interest politics" (Rugg and Nye 2012).

While political leaders sparred over gun laws, Mark Barden and Nicole Hockley—both parents of children killed in the Newtown shooting—launched Sandy Hook Promise, a nonprofit organization aimed at teaching people about the causes of gun violence and providing them with tools to help prevent it. The organization invited supporters to pledge "to do all I can to protect children from gun violence by encouraging and supporting solutions that create safer, healthier homes, schools and communities." Some of the programs sponsored by Sandy Hook Promise include "Know the Signs," which trains people to recognize an individual who may be at risk of violence; "Say Something," which provides an anonymous reporting system for potential violence; and "Start with Hello," which encourages students to reach out to classmates who experience chronic social isolation.

An unfortunate outgrowth of the intense debate over gun rights that followed the Sandy Hook shooting was the propagation of conspiracy theories about the incident. The most extreme of these theories claimed that the shooting was an elaborate hoax perpetuated by the Obama administration, gun control advocates, or other powerful entities in order to increase public support for a federal assault weapons ban. "Hoaxers," most of whom tended to hold strong antigovernment or progun views, seized on minor discrepancies in media reports or official statements to support their spurious claims. Videos promoting rumors and falsehoods about the shooting received millions of views online, and some people who believed these accounts harassed or threatened the Sandy Hook families.

Even though all of the major conspiracy narratives were repeatedly debunked by reputable sources, they continued to circulate online and traumatize survivors of the shooting. Leonard Pozner, whose six-year-old son Noah was killed in the massacre, responded by forming the HONR Network, a volunteer organization that works with Internet providers to monitor and remove hoaxer posts and videos. In August 2018, the families of nine Sandy Hook victims filed a defamation lawsuit against InfoWars host Alex Jones. The suit argued that Jones made false claims about the shooting on social media and encouraged his followers to harass and threaten the families online.

Further Reading

Childress, Sarah. 2013. "How the Gun-Rights Lobby Won after Newtown." PBS Frontline, December 10, 2013. https://www.pbs.org/wgbh/frontline/article /how-the-gun-rights-lobby-won-after-newtown/.

Drake, Bruce. 2013. "A Year after Newtown, Little Change in Public Opinion on Guns." Pew Research Center, December 12, 2013. http://www.pew research.org/fact-tank/2013/12/12/a-year-after-newtown-little-change -in-public-opinion-on-guns/.

Obama, Barack. 2012. "Statement by the President on the School Shooting in Newtown, Connecticut." White House, December 14, 2012. https://obama whitehouse.archives.gov/the-press-office/2012/12/14/statement-president -school-shooting-newtown-ct.

Obama, Barack. 2016. "The Obama Years, Part 3: Just Like Anyone Else's Kids." History Channel. https://www.history.com/the-obama-years/newtown.html.

Rugg, Peter, and James Nye. 2012. "'The Most Revolting, Tone Deaf Statement I've Ever Seen': NRA Condemned after Its Astonishing Response to Sandy Hook Massacre Calling for Schools to Arm Themselves." Daily Mail, December 21, 2012. http://www.dailymail.co.uk/news/article-2251762 /NRA-condemned-astonishing-response-Sandy-Hook-massacre-calling -schools-arm-themselves.html.

Sedensky, Stephen J., III. 2013. "Report of the State's Attorney for the Judicial District of Danbury on the Shootings at Sandy Hook Elementary School." State of Connecticut, November 25, 2013. http://www.ct.gov/csao/lib /csao/Sandy_Hook_Final_Report.pdf.

The Umpqua Community College Shooting (2015)

When a gunman killed eight students and an assistant professor at Umpqua Community College (UCC) in Oregon on October 1, 2015, the incident bore many similarities to previous school shootings. The perpetrator was socially isolated, showed signs of mental illness, had access to firearms at home, idolized mass shooters, and viewed violence as a way to achieve notoriety. The response to the shooting also mirrored previous incidents, with calls for new gun control laws met with staunch resistance by the powerful gun rights lobby. "Somehow this has become routine. The reporting is routine. My response here at this podium ends up being routine, the conversation in the aftermath of it. We've become numb to this," said President Barack Obama. "Our thoughts and prayers are not enough. It's not enough. It does not capture the heartache and grief and anger that we should feel, and it does nothing to prevent this carnage from being inflicted someplace else in America—next week, or a couple months from now" (Ford and Payne 2015).

The Incident

UCC serves around 3,300 students on a picturesque campus located about 70 miles south of Eugene, Oregon. On the second day of fall classes in 2015, a 26-year-old student named Chris Harper-Mercer walked into his introductory composition class in Snyder Hall shortly after 10:30 a.m. He wore a flak jacket and carried five handguns, a semiautomatic rifle, and multiple ammunition magazines. After fatally shooting the instructor at point-blank range, the gunman handed a computer flash drive to one student and told him to go to the back of the room. The gunman then began shooting other students one by one, sometimes laughing or taunting them as he did so. According to some witnesses, the shooter asked several students if they were Christians before he shot them.

At 10:44 a.m., when two police officers arrived on the scene, the gunman stepped into the hallway and fired at them. The officers returned fire and wounded the gunman, who then ducked back into the classroom and shot himself in the head. By the time he died, the shooter had killed 9 people and wounded 8 others, including Chris Mintz, a UCC student and U.S. Army veteran who was shot several times while working to evacuate nearby classrooms and help the wounded. Mintz was released from the hospital within a week and received several commendations for his courageous actions.

The Aftermath

On the USB drive the shooter gave to a fellow student, police investigators found a six-page written manifesto in which he expressed anger at society and despondence over having "no job, no life, no successes" (Coffman 2017). He also claimed to be aligned with demonic forces and said that he was destined to enjoy a hero's welcome in Hell. In interviews with the shooter's mother and other people who knew him, police learned that he had been diagnosed as being on the autism spectrum. Some sources described him as hate-filled, socially isolated, and obsessed with mass shootings. He downloaded videos depicting murders and expressed admiration for the perpetrators of the school shootings at Columbine High School in Colorado and Sandy Hook Elementary School in Connecticut.

In addition to the six firearms recovered from Snyder Hall, police found eight other firearms at the shooter's home. They noted that all of the guns had been purchased legally by the perpetrator or members of his family. In the wake of the UCC shooting, many critics questioned how a person with serious mental health issues could have been allowed to purchase firearms. Both federal and state law only prohibited gun sales to individuals who had been involuntarily committed for inpatient treatment at a psychiatric care facility. Since the UCC shooter had never received that level of treatment, he was legally permitted to purchase firearms. Gun control advocates called on Congress to close this loophole and strengthen the criminal background check system in order to keep guns out of the hands of mentally unstable individuals. In 2017, Oregon passed a law that allowed family members or law enforcement officials to request an Extreme Risk Protection Order from a state court to temporarily block potentially dangerous individuals from purchasing or possessing firearms. Supporters claimed that the law might have stopped the UCC shooter if it had been in place at the time.

At the federal level, calls for legislation to prevent gun violence encountered stiff opposition from gun rights supporters and failed to gain traction in Congress. When asked about the UCC shooting, several candidates for the 2016 Republican presidential nomination argued that passing new gun control laws was not an effective response to mass shootings. "I keep waiting for someone to tell me what new gun law we can pass that would have prevented this shooting or Sandy Hook or Aurora or Charleston," said former Arkansas governor Mike Huckabee. "Just tell me what gun law that is because I've yet to have somebody tell me what that is." U.S. senator Marco Rubio of Florida claimed that such measures were pointless because "criminals don't follow gun laws. Only law-abiding people follow gun laws" (Bixby 2015).

Further Reading

Bixby, Scott. 2015. "30 Years after Banning the Sale of Machine Guns, Here's How Easy It Is to Buy One." Mic, October 19, 2015. https://mic.com /articles/126943/30-years-after-banning-the-sale-of-machine-guns-here -s-how-easy-it-is-to-buy-one#.2rfVedAQH.

Coffman, Keith. 2017. "Oregon College Shooter Wrote of Kinship with Mass Killers in Manifesto." Reuters, September 8, 2017. https://www.reuters .com/article/us-usa-shooting-oregon/oregon-college-shooter-wrote-of -kinship-with-mass-killers-in-manifesto-idUSKCN1BJ2QK.

Ford, Dana, and Ed Payne. 2015. "Oregon Shooting: Gunman Dead after College Rampage." CNN, October 2, 2015. https://www.cnn.com/2015/10/01/us /oregon-college-shooting/index.html.

Theen, Andrew. 2017. "Umpqua Community College Shooting: Killer's Manifesto Reveals Racist, Satanic Views." The Oregonian, September 8, 2017. https://www.oregonlive.com/pacific-northwest-news/index.ssf/2017/09 /umpqua_community_college_shoot_3.html.

The Las Vegas Shooting (2017)

On October 1, 2017, a gunman concealed in a high-rise hotel suite on the famous Las Vegas Strip opened fire on a crowd of 22,000 people attending an open-air concert below. Fifty-eight people were killed and 400 others were wounded, making it the deadliest mass shooting in U.S. history. The Las Vegas shooting occurred less than 16 months after what had previously been considered the deadliest mass shooting—a terrorist rampage at a nightclub in Orlando, Florida, that killed 49 people and left 53 others injured. Along with mass shootings that claimed the lives of 35 people at churches in Charleston, South Carolina, and Sutherland Springs, Texas, these events left many Americans feeling under siege from a steady barrage of gun violence. Although each incident generated public demands for stricter gun control laws, gun rights advocates consistently blocked efforts to pass new legislation at both the state and federal levels.

The Incident

The Las Vegas shooting took place during the Route 91 Harvest Festival, a three-day concert held on a 15-acre lot at the south end of the Strip. The popular event, which was in its fourth year in 2017, featured performances by many well-known country music artists against the backdrop of the glittering city skyline. The concert venue was located diagonally across the street from the Mandalay Bay resort hotel, where a 64-year-old retired accountant and high-stakes gambler named Stephen Paddock rented a suite of rooms on the 32nd floor overlooking the festival grounds. The perpetrator spent several days acquiring more than two dozen guns—including 14 AR-15 semiautomatic rifles equipped with 100-round magazines and modified with bump stocks to increase their firing rate to that of a fully automatic weapon—and transporting them up to the rooms in large suitcases, sometimes with the help of unaware hotel staff.

At around 10:00 p.m. local time on October 1, a hotel security guard responded to a complaint indicating that an access door to the 32nd floor had been bolted shut. Upon investigating further, he heard drilling sounds coming from Paddock's suite and knocked on the door. The gunman shot through the door and injured the security guard, who radioed for help. At 10:05 p.m., the perpetrator broke two outer windows with a hammer and began firing into the crowd of concertgoers below. Many people were confused at first, mistaking the sound of gunfire for fireworks or pyrotechnics from festival headliner Jason Aldean's set. Upon realizing the danger, the crowd began to panic, with thousands of people frantically running for cover and trying to break through the security fences surrounding the lot. Las Vegas police officers came under fire as they tried to evacuate the concert venue, assist the wounded, and locate the shooter.

The perpetrator fired more than 1,100 rounds in 10 minutes. The shooting stopped at 10:15 p.m. as police arrived at the Mandalay Bay in response to the call from the security guard. When the authorities reached the gunman's suite, they found him dead from a self-inflicted gunshot wound. Fifty-eight people died and 851 were injured—about half from gunfire and the rest from trying to escape the chaotic scene. The terror and panic that overtook the crowd was documented in extensive video footage from surveillance cameras, police body cams, and cell phones belonging to concertgoers. Most of the videos eventually appeared online, where they compounded the trauma experienced by survivors and gave rise to countless conspiracy theories about the incident. Investigators never uncovered a motive for the shooting, and they noted that the perpetrator had no criminal record or history of mental illness. They did learn that the gunman had been stockpiling weapons and researching outdoor concerts in Boston, Chicago, and Las Vegas for six months beforehand.

The Aftermath

The Las Vegas shooting was the deadliest in a series of high-profile mass shootings in public places across the United States within the span of a few years. Although the incidents differed in many respects, they combined to create a sense of increasing vulnerability to gun violence in the minds of many Americans. On June 17, 2015, for instance, a 21-year-old white supremacist named Dylann Roof fatally shot nine African American parishioners in a Bible study group at the historic Emanuel African Methodist Episcopal Church in Charleston, South Carolina. The perpetrator used a .45-caliber Glock semiautomatic handgun that he was mistakenly allowed to purchase, despite facing a felony charge from a previous arrest, due to a breakdown in the criminal background check system maintained by the Federal Bureau of Investigation (FBI). In a confession, he said that he intended his actions to start a race war and lead to resegregation of the South. The perpetrator was eventually convicted on federal hate crimes charges and sentenced to death by lethal injection.

Much of the public discussion in the wake of the Charleston shooting focused on shoring up the federal background check system to prevent people with a history of mental illness from purchasing guns. "Once again innocent people were killed in part because someone who wanted to inflict harm had no trouble getting their hands on a gun," said President Barack Obama. "At some point we will have to deal with the fact that this kind of mass violence doesn't happen in other countries and it is in our power to do something about it" (Roberts 2015). Efforts to introduce stricter gun control measures met with strong opposition, however, and failed to gain traction in Congress. Gun rights advocates argued that lawmakers should work to improve mental health care and crack down on hate groups rather than making it more difficult for law-abiding citizens to protect themselves.

On June 12, 2016—less than a year after the Charleston shooting—29-year-old Omar Mateen perpetrated the deadliest U.S. mass shooting until that time at Pulse, a gay nightclub in Orlando, Florida. The shooter killed 49 people and wounded 53 others before law enforcement officers killed him following a three-hour hostage negotiation. Initial news reports claimed that the shooter intentionally targeted Pulse because of its gay clientele and described the attack as an anti-LGBTQ hate crime. Later interviews and evidence suggested, however, that the shooter may have picked the nightclub randomly, without realizing it was a gay bar, after failing to gain access to a college and other potential targets. Federal authorities eventually classified the shooting as a terrorist attack because the perpetrator swore allegiance to the Islamic State of Iraq and Syria, more commonly known as ISIS, and proclaimed his motive to be revenge for U.S. military bombings in Iraq and Syria.

Once again, questions arose as to how to prevent dangerous individuals from purchasing firearms. Mateen bought a semiautomatic rifle and several large-capacity magazines legally in the weeks before the shooting, despite the fact that he had appeared on the FBI's terrorist watch list until 2014. Democratic members of the U.S. Senate introduced legislation to require the FBI to include suspected terrorists in the national background check database to prevent them from buying guns, but the bill failed to pass. Opponents argued that the measure would have hampered antiterrorism efforts by alerting individuals that they were under FBI surveillance.

The Orlando nightclub shooting also drew national attention to Florida's permissive gun laws, including its controversial stand-your-ground statute, which gives citizens broad latitude to use deadly force in self-defense if they have reason to believe their life is in danger. Gun control advocates failed to pass any reform measures after the Pulse shooting, and several state lawmakers expressed satisfaction about defeating proposed legislation that would have expanded the list of places Florida residents could carry guns to include airports, college campuses, and government buildings. "All of the bills that the gun lobby pushed was [sic] defeated," said Democratic state representative Carlos Guillermo-Smith. "It's a win. They didn't get anything they wanted in this last legislature, which is kind of a sea change. I know that Pulse was a reason" (Mindock 2017). Florida gun supporters vowed to continue pushing for new state laws to protect the Second Amendment rights of law-abiding citizens. They achieved a major victory in 2017, when Republican governor Rick Scott signed legislation that strengthened the stand-your-ground law by requiring prosecutors to provide "clear and convincing evidence" that a citizen involved in a shooting had a motive other than self-defense.

About a month after the Las Vegas shooting, another church shooting sent the nation reeling once again. On November 5, 2017, a gunman identified as 26-year-old Devin Patrick Kelley killed 26 people—nearly half of them children—and injured 20 others who were attending services at the First Baptist Church in Sutherland Springs, Texas, a small town about 30 miles east of San Antonio. As the gunman left the building, he was shot and wounded by Stephen Willeford, a nearby homeowner and former firearms instructor who had responded to the sound of gunfire by grabbing his AR-15 semiautomatic rifle and running outside. When the perpetrator fled the scene in his vehicle, Willeford and a friend followed and engaged in a high-speed chase until the perpetrator crashed. By the time law enforcement arrived on the scene, they found the perpetrator dead of a self-inflicted gunshot wound.

An investigation revealed that the perpetrator should have been prohibited from purchasing firearms due to a domestic violence conviction that led to his discharge from the military. The U.S. Air Force failed to report the offense to the FBI, however, so it did not appear in the National Instant Criminal Background Check System (NICS). Within a few days of the church shooting, Republican U.S. senator John Cornyn of Texas proposed legislation he called the Fix NICS Act to provide incentives for state and federal agencies to improve their reporting procedures. Although the measure's progress stalled for several months, proponents eventually attached it to the omnibus spending bill signed into law by President Donald Trump in March 2018.

Gun control advocates asserted that addressing shortcomings in the federal background check system was insufficient to solve the problem of mass shootings. They pushed for legislation that would prohibit the sale of large-capacity magazines capable of holding more than 10 rounds of ammunition, for instance, or ban the sale of bump stocks that increased the firing rate of semiautomatic weapons. Gun rights activists resisted such measures, which they claimed would only prevent law-abiding citizens from obtaining weapons for self-defense. They contended that the Texas church shooting could have been much worse if the neighbor who responded had been unarmed. Many local people who were affected by the massacre adopted this view. New applications for gun licenses increased by 167 percent in Sutherland Springs and the surrounding county in the month following the shooting. "Sutherland Springs may not be a town you want to mess with anymore," said Willeford of the increase in gun ownership (Montgomery 2018).

Further Reading

Bui, Lynn, Matt Zapotosky, Devlin Barrett, and Mark Berman. 2017. "At Least 59 Killed in Las Vegas Shooting Rampage, More Than 500 Others Injured." *Washington Post,* October 17, 2017. https://www.washingtonpost.com /news/morning-mix/wp/2017/10/02/police-shut-down-part-of-las-vegas -strip-due-to-shooting/?utm_term=.ea7d16853ea3.

Mindock, Clark. 2017. "Gun Control Efforts Stalled in Orlando Following Largest Mass Shooting in U.S. History." Independent, June 11, 2017. https:// www.independent.co.uk/news/world/americas/florida-gun-control -laws-orlando-pulse-nightclub-shooting-a7785061.html.

Montgomery, David. 2018. "Sutherland Springs, Seven Months Later." *Houston Chronicle,* June 13, 2018. https://www.houstonchronicle.com/local/gray

-matters/article/sutherland-springs-texas-church-shooting-12988751
.php.

Roberts, Dan. 2015. "Charleston Church Shooting: Obama Calls for Gun Control in Wake of Tragedy." *The Guardian,* June 18, 2015. https://www.the
guardian.com/us-news/2015/jun/18/charleston-church-shooting-obama
-calls-gun-control.

The Marjory Stoneman Douglas High School Shooting (2018)

The school shooting that launched the student-led Never Again movement occurred on February 14, 2018, at Marjory Stoneman Douglas High School (MSD) in Parkland, Florida. A former student armed with an assault rifle murdered 17 people and wounded 17 others in a six-minute shooting rampage. Student survivors of the MSD shooting quickly emerged as leading voices in the gun violence prevention movement. They demanded meaningful legislative action to prevent future school shootings, and they vowed to mobilize young voters to defeat elected officials who accepted donations from the National Rifle Association (NRA). Much of the student organizing took place on social media using the hashtag #NeverAgain, and it culminated in the March for Our Lives, which attracted an estimated 2 million participants to demonstrations in Washington, D.C., and 800 other locations in the United States and around the world.

The Incident

As part of the Broward County Public School District, MSD High School serves over 3,000 students from Parkland—an affluent suburb of Fort Lauderdale—and nearby Coral Springs. The school is named after the famous writer and conservationist Marjory Stoneman Douglas (1890–1998), who fought to protect the Everglades from development. On February 14, 2018, 19-year-old Nikolas Cruz was dropped off at the MSD campus by an Uber driver at 2:19 p.m. A staff member saw him walking toward a building carrying a duffle bag and wearing a backpack and recognized him as a former student who had been expelled from MSD for disciplinary reasons. The staff member radioed to warn a colleague but did not issue a campus-wide security alert.

At 2:21 p.m., shortly before MSD students were dismissed for the day, the perpetrator entered Building 12 and removed an AR-15 semiautomatic rifle and several magazines of ammunition from his bag. He then pulled a fire alarm and began shooting students and staff members who emerged from classrooms. Upon hearing gunshots, many classrooms implemented emergency lockdown procedures, in which students barricaded doorways, took cover under desks, or hid in closets or bathrooms. At about 2:24, the gunman went up to the third floor and continued shooting for three more minutes. He then dropped his weapon and escaped by joining the crowd of panicked students fleeing the school. The shooting lasted for six minutes, during which the gunman killed 11 people on the first floor and 6 people on the third floor. Although an armed school resource officer from the Broward County Sheriff Department was on campus, he remained outside Building 12 for the duration of the shooting. The officer later said that he mistakenly thought the perpetrator was a sniper firing out a window of the building.

After leaving the MSD grounds, the perpetrator purchased a soft drink from a Subway restaurant located inside a nearby Walmart store, then walked to a McDonald's. He was apprehended around 3:40 p.m. while wandering around a Coral Springs neighborhood about two miles away from the school. He was positively identified from surveillance videos taken by school security cameras as well as by eyewitnesses to the shooting. After being taken into custody, he confessed to the crime and was charged with 17 counts of premeditated murder. Broward County Sheriff Department officials soon revealed that they had received several calls from concerned citizens in the previous two years alleging that the perpetrator had threatened to shoot up a school. In addition, the Federal Bureau of Investigation had received tips about the shooter making threatening statements on social media, but the complaints were not referred to local agents for follow-up.

The Aftermath

The MSD tragedy surpassed the 1999 Columbine High School massacre as the deadliest shooting ever to occur at an American high school. The attack took place within a few months of deadly mass shootings at an outdoor concert in Las Vegas, Nevada, and at a Baptist church in Sutherland Springs, Texas. The proximity of these events helped to focus public attention on the prevalence of gun violence and create a receptive atmosphere for change. Student survivors of the MSD shooting quickly stepped into the role of change agents. Calling themselves the "mass shooting generation," they described coming of age in a post-Columbine environment of active-shooter drills, campus security protocols, and constant vigilance. "We all grew up with Sandy Hook and terrorism and code-red active-shooter drills," said MSD senior David Hogg. "We have all grown up conditioned to be afraid. And we're all sick and tired of being afraid" (Hogg 2018, 19).

As the national media descended on Parkland in the wake of the shooting, the student survivors used the platform to express exasperation with what they viewed as government leaders' inability or unwillingness to break the cycle of gun violence. The student activists gave interviews, made speeches, published editorials, participated in a televised CNN town hall, and met with state lawmakers to demand meaningful action to promote school safety. Many students focused their anger on the political influence wielded by the NRA and other powerful gun rights organizations. "If all our government and president can do is send thoughts and prayers, then it's time for victims to be the change that we need to see," declared MSD senior Emma González at a gun control rally in Fort Lauderdale a few days after the shooting. "Politicians who sit in their gilded House and Senate seats funded by the NRA telling us nothing could have been done to prevent this, we call BS. They say tougher guns laws do not decrease gun violence. We call BS. They say a good guy with a gun stops a bad guy with a gun. We call BS. . . . That us kids don't know what we're talking about, that we're too young to understand how the government works. We call BS" (CNN Staff 2018).

The Parkland students employed social media as an effective tool in disseminating their message, shaming opponents, and silencing critics. In the aftermath of the shooting, González opened a Twitter account with the handle @Emma4Change and quickly accumulated 1.6 million followers—more than twice as many as the NRA. "People always say, 'Get off your phones,' but social media is our weapon," said MSD junior class president Jaclyn Corin. "Without it, the movement wouldn't have spread this fast" (Alter 2018). The student activists' social media presence featured a unique combination of youthful innocence and idealism, righteous indignation and outrage, and adolescent humor and sarcasm that disarmed their enemies and brought new energy to the decades-old gun control debate. "They're using Twitter as a means to ridicule, to dismiss, to brush past the usual criticisms and just say, 'These people are full of it,'" said gun policy expert Robert Spitzer (Alter 2018).

Some right-wing media personalities and gun rights extremists attempted to discredit the Parkland students by promoting conspiracy theories about the MSD shooting. They claimed, for instance, that the outspoken student survivors were "crisis actors" who were being manipulated by powerful liberal antigun interests to exploit the tragedy for political gain. Some critics posted doctored images and GIFs online that appeared to show González tearing up a copy of the U.S. Constitution. The real images came from footage showing her ripping a shooting-range target. When the student activists pushed back against such misinformation on social media, their responses went viral. Millions of young Twitter followers rallied to their defense, generating a massive online backlash against their conservative critics.

After Leslie Gibson, a Republican candidate for a seat in the Maine legislature, referred to González as a "skinhead lesbian" on Twitter, he faced such an outpouring of criticism that he was forced to withdraw from the race. When conservative talk show host Laura Ingraham mocked Hogg on Twitter by posting a list of colleges that had supposedly rejected his applications for admission, Hogg responded by posting a list of her advertisers, which resulted in boycotts that convinced two dozen companies to drop their support for her program. The Parkland teens also used social media to pressure dozens of large companies—including MetLife, Hertz, Avis, Delta Airlines, and Wyndham Hotels—to sever business relationships with the NRA and stop offering discounts to NRA members.

The Parkland students' gun reform advocacy prompted a shift in public opinion. The percentage of Americans who expressed support for stronger gun regulations grew to 68 percent—an increase of 8 percent from a poll taken three months before the MSD shooting—while the percentage who expressed support for the NRA declined to 37 percent (Alter 2018). The mainstream media took note of these changes and speculated about whether the student activists might break through the national impasse over gun control. "On the surface, they're not so different from previous generations of idealistic teenagers who set out to change the world, only to find it is not so easy," Charlotte Alter wrote in a March 2018 *Time* magazine cover story. "Yet over the past month, these students have become the central organizers of what may turn out to be the most powerful grassroots gun-reform movement in nearly two decades" (Alter 2018).

Pressure from the Parkland students helped produce major new gun legislation in Florida, which has historically been considered one of the most gun-friendly states. The MSD High School Public Safety Act, which passed on March 9 with the votes of 67 Republican legislators endorsed by the NRA, increased the minimum age for firearm purchases from 18 to 21, established mandatory waiting periods and criminal background checks, prohibited people deemed mentally unstable or potentially violent from purchasing guns, banned the sale of bump stocks that increase the firing rate of semiautomatic weapons, and allocated funds for increasing police presence at schools or arming staff members. Although the law did not address all of the concerns expressed by the student activists, it marked the first time in two decades that Florida lawmakers increased gun regulations.

Survivors of the MSD shooting also joined forces with Women's March youth groups to organize the National School Walkout. During the planning stages, administrators at some high schools threatened to suspend students who left class to participate in the demonstration against school shootings. In response, hundreds of U.S. colleges and universities—including Columbia University, Harvard University, the University of Florida, and Yale University—announced that students who faced disciplinary action for taking part in peaceful protests would not jeopardize their chances of admission. On March 14, nearly 1 million students from more than 3,000 schools nationwide left class for 17 minutes in remembrance of the Parkland victims. It was the largest demonstration against gun violence in U.S. history until that time. The MSD student activists continued to advocate for gun control at the national level through the #NeverAgain campaign, which culminated in an even larger demonstration 10 days later with the March for Our Lives.

Further Reading

Alter, Charlotte. 2018. "The School Shooting Generation Has Had Enough." *Time,* March 22, 2018. http://time.com/longform/never-again-movement/.

CNN Staff. 2018. "Florida Student Emma González to Lawmakers and Gun Advocates: 'We Call BS.'" CNN, February 17, 2018. https://www.cnn.com /2018/02/17/us/florida-student-emma-gonzalez-speech/index.html.

Cottle, Michelle. 2018. "How Parkland Students Changed the Gun Debate." *The Atlantic,* February 28, 2018. https://www.theatlantic.com/politics/archive /2018/02/parkland-students-power/554399/.

Hogg, David, and Lauren Hogg. 2018. *#Never Again: A New Generation Draws the Line.* New York: Random House.

Witt, Emily. 2018. "How the Survivors of Parkland Began the Never Again Movement." *New Yorker,* February 19, 2018. https://www.newyorker.com/news /news-desk/how-the-survivors-of-parkland-began-the-never-again -movement.

The Never Again Movement Forms (2018)

Within days of the February 14 mass shooting at Marjory Stoneman Douglas (MSD) High School in Parkland, Florida, a group of student survivors formed Never Again MSD, a political action committee that advocates for stricter gun control regulations with the goal of preventing future school shootings. Using the hashtag #NeverAgain, the student activists launched a social media campaign demanding legislative action aimed at reducing gun violence. They expressed support for such measures as increasing the federal minimum age for gun ownership to 21, requiring universal background checks for gun purchases, restoring the federal assault weapons ban, and prohibiting the sale of high-capacity ammunition magazines. The students also criticized politicians who accepted campaign contributions from the National Rifle Association (NRA) and organized youth voter registration drives aimed at voting those politicians out of office.

The Parkland Students Organize

In the midst of their shock, grief, and anger about the murder of 17 of their classmates and teachers, many MSD students felt a sense of obligation to remember the dead by speaking out against gun violence and taking action to prevent other people from becoming victims. When the media converged on Parkland in the aftermath of the shooting, many students gave interviews in which they called on political leaders to pass stricter gun control laws. Some students condemned the NRA's influence over American politics, which they viewed as being responsible for lawmakers' inaction following previous school shootings. "This is how I'm dealing with my grief," MSD senior Emma González explained. "The thing that caused me grief, the thing that had no right to cause me grief, the thing that had no right to happen in the first place, I have to do something actively to prevent it from happening to somebody else" (Witt 2018).

After attending a candlelight vigil on February 15, student Cameron Kasky invited his friends Alex Wind and Sofie Whitney to his house to develop a plan of action. "The day after the shooting, we said something needs to happen," Wind recalled. "There needs to be a central space; there needs to be a movement" (Lowery 2018). The three teenagers stayed up all night discussing ways to confront the issue of gun violence. Kasky came up with the name "Never Again" to describe their campaign and used the #NeverAgain hashtag in a Facebook post. On February 17, Kasky and other MSD survivors attended a gun control rally at the Broward County Federal Courthouse in Fort Lauderdale. González delivered a fiery 11-minute speech in which she rejected the "thoughts and prayers" offered by President Donald Trump and other Republican political leaders. She concluded by leading the assembled crowd in a call-and-response of "We call BS" on the reasons typically cited by lawmakers for failing to make meaningful reforms to the nation's gun laws.

Kasky recruited González and several other classmates who spoke at the rally, including David Hogg and Delaney Tarr, to help launch the Never Again campaign. Other students quickly joined after learning about the group, including Jaclyn Corin, Sarah Chadwick, Alfonso Calderon, and Ryan Deitsch. Tarr described the students' motivations in an opinion article for *Teen Vogue* magazine. "Our childhoods may have been stolen from us, but there are so many lives that can still be protected and saved. Just because this has happened to many before us does not mean it must continue to happen to those after," she wrote. "Every kid, every person, deserves to feel safe wherever they go, especially at school. That is why we are marching and making ourselves heard. Knowing that we can keep this from happening to even one more person is the only thing that makes me feel even a little bit better about living through this senseless tragedy. . . . We are no longer just high school students, that much is true. We are now the future, we are a movement, we are the change" (Tarr 2018).

The student organizers of Never Again MSD created Facebook and Twitter accounts that quickly gained thousands of followers. They formed a political action committee and set up a headquarters in donated office space in a strip mall. On February 18, they announced plans for a nation-wide student-led demonstration against gun violence—the March for Our Lives—to be held in Washington, D.C., on March 24. They also developed a list of policy goals that included universal background checks for firearm purchases, a ban on the sale of assault weapons and high-capacity ammunition magazines, and government funding for research into gun violence prevention. The student activists recognized that their movement faced powerful opposition, but they insisted that the young people would win in the long run. "This fight is not going to be easy. This fight is not going to be short," Hogg acknowledged. "The people and the special interests who want to pass gun laws and make it easier for people to get guns are not going to stop—and we can't either" (Seelinger 2018).

Never Again Becomes a National Movement

On February 20, Never Again activists Jaclyn Corin and Sofie Whitney helped organize a trip by 100 MSD student survivors to the Florida State Capitol in Tallahassee. The group met with state lawmakers to voice their concerns about school shootings and demand action on gun control. To their disappointment, however, they also watched from the gallery as legislators decisively voted down a bill that would have banned assault weapons, such as the AR-15–style semiautomatic rifle used by the perpetrator of the Parkland shooting. A few weeks later, on March 9, the student protesters achieved what a *Washington Post* editorial called a "stunning" victory over the NRA when Florida lawmakers passed the MSD High School Public Safety Act—the first gun control legislation to be approved in the state in 20 years. "It is now beyond doubt: The fearless student survivors of the Parkland, Florida, mass shooting are changing the debate about gun control," the editorial stated (Editorial Board 2018).

As the March for Our Lives gathered momentum, the Never Again teen organizers gained national prominence. The March 22 issue of *Time* magazine featured a photograph of Corin, González, Hogg, Kasky, and Wind on the cover. A growing list of celebrities voiced support for the movement, pledged to participate in the march, or donated money to the cause. George and Amal Clooney, Oprah Winfrey, and Steven Spielberg contributed $500,000 each to aid in the students' organizing efforts. Many people made smaller donations on a GoFundMe page set up by Never Again MSD or signed the group's online petition demanding that Congress pass gun control legislation. Barack and Michelle Obama sent a handwritten letter to the Parkland students expressing support and admiration for their work to end gun violence. "You've helped awaken the conscience of the nation, and challenged decision-makers to make the safety of our children the country's top priority," they wrote. "Throughout our history, young people like you have led the way in making America better" (Gstalter 2018).

As the Never Again movement expanded, the student activists increasingly emphasized the importance of mobilizing young voters in order to counteract the NRA's influence on American politics and elect candidates who favored gun control measures. "The world failed us," Kasky stated, "and we're here to make a new one that's going to be easier on the next generation. If you're against that, then get out" (Alter 2018). In response to gun rights advocates who claimed that passing new gun laws would not prevent mass shootings, the Never Again activists pointed out that lax gun laws had enabled the perpetrator of the MSD shooting—who had documented behavioral and mental health issues and had threatened to harm others—to acquire a weapon intended for military combat. "Nikolas Cruz, the shooter at my school, was reported to the police thirty-nine times," said Calderon. "We have to vote people out who have been paid for by the NRA. They're allowing this to happen. They're making it easier for people like Nick Cruz to acquire an AR-15" (Witt 2018).

In June 2018 Never Again activists embarked on a bus tour of the United States, with stops scheduled in 70 cities where the NRA spent the most money to gain political influence, to encourage young people to register to vote. Since the Republican-controlled Congress appeared unlikely to pass gun control legislation, the students aimed to unseat its members in the 2018 midterm elections. "We've sat around for too long being inactive in our political climate, and children have died," Hogg declared. "It's time for us to stand up and take action and hold our elected officials responsible, and if our elected officials are not willing to stand up and say, 'I'm not willing to take money for the NRA, because children are dying,' they shouldn't be in office, and they won't be in office, because this is a midterm year, and this is the change that we need" (Durkee 2018).

Looking even further ahead, the teens pointed out that members of their generation would eventually become the nation's leaders. They foresaw a cultural shift in attitudes toward gun control and the NRA and predicted that they would eventually succeed in breaking the cycle of gun violence and achieving positive change. "Regardless of what your opinions are or where you come from, you need to realize we are the future of America. And if you choose not to stand with us, that's OK because you'll be on the wrong side of the history textbooks that we write," Hogg stated. "We can and we will outlive our opponents because they're old, and they are stuck in their old ways. We will change the face of America with or without our opponents" (Simon 2018).

Further Reading

Alter, Charlotte. 2018. "The School Shooting Generation Has Had Enough." *Time,* March 22, 2018. http://time.com/longform/never-again-movement/.

Cottle, Michelle. 2018. "How Parkland Students Changed the Gun Debate." *Atlantic,* February 28, 2018. https://www.theatlantic.com/politics/archive /2018/02/parkland-students-power/554399/.

Durkee, Alison. 2018. "March for Our Lives: What to Know about the Nationwide March Led by the Parkland Survivors." *Mic,* February 18, 2018. https:// mic.com/articles/188034/march-for-our-lives-what-to-know-about-the -nationwide-march-led-by-the-parkland-survivors#.ask70VGz2.

Editorial Board. 2018. "A Rarity for the NRA: Defeat." *Washington Post,* March 8, 2018. https://www.washingtonpost.com/opinions/a-rarity-for-the-nra-de feat/2018/03/08/0ec683dc-2309-11e8-badd-7c9f29a55815_story.html ?noredirect=on&utm_term=.712eabb3b71d.

Gstalter, Morgan. 2018. "Obamas Send Handwritten Note to Parkland Students: 'We Will Be There for You.'" The Hill, March 21, 2018. https://thehill .com/blogs/blog-briefing-room/news/379539-obamas-send-handwritten -note-to-parkland-students-we-will-be.

Lowery, Wesley. 2018. "He Survived the Florida School Shooting. He Vows Not to Return to Classes until Gun Laws Change." *Washington Post,* February 18, 2018. https://www.washingtonpost.com/news/post-nation/wp/2018 /02/18/students-organize-to-fight-for-gun-law-changes/?noredirect=on &utm_term=.e736858f55ba.

Seelinger, Lani. 2018. "What Is Never Again MSD? Parkland Survivors Are Standing Up to Politicians and the NRA." Bustle, February 19, 2018.

https://www.bustle.com/p/what-is-never-again-msd-parkland-survivors
-are-standing-up-to-politicians-the-nra-8262680.

Simon, Scott. 2018. "Parkland Student David Hogg on the Gun Control Movement Led by Teens." National Public Radio, March 24, 2018. https://
www.npr.org/2018/03/24/596647455/parkland-student-david-hogg-on
-the-gun-control-movement-driven-by-teens.

Tarr, Delaney. 2018. "I Survived the Parkland Shooting. This Is What I Want
Everyone to Know." Teen Vogue, February 19, 2018. https://www.teen
vogue.com/story/i-survived-the-parkland-shooting-delaney-tarr?verso
=true.

Witt, Emily. 2018. "How the Survivors of Parkland Began the Never Again Movement." *New Yorker,* February 19, 2018. https://www.newyorker.com
/news/news-desk/how-the-survivors-of-parkland-began-the-never-again
-movement.

The March for Our Lives (2018)

By 2018, the response to mass shootings in the United States seemed
to follow a predictable pattern. Shootings at Columbine High School in
1999, Virginia Tech University in 2007, and Sandy Hook Elementary
School in 2012 initially elicited an outpouring of public concern about
gun violence and demands for new restrictions on firearms. Each time,
however, gun rights supporters deflected blame away from guns and
called for improvements to mental health care, outreach for disaffected
and potentially violent youths, increased school security, or bans on violent video games. Within a few weeks, the media shifted its focus away
from the victims and their families, the pressure to pass new gun control
legislation faded, and the status quo remained in place until the next
mass shooting occurred. "This seemingly never-ending cycle has been
deemed 'inevitable' in the minds of Americans, and learned helplessness
has allowed this epidemic to spiral out of control," said student activist
Jaclyn Corin. "Citizens can only feel hopeless as they sit in their living
rooms, watching headlines of *another* mass shooting flash across their
screens. People often send thoughts and prayers but eventually shrug it
off, firmly believing that there was nothing they could do to prevent this
tragedy from occurring" (Corin 2018).

The pattern showed signs of disruption following the February 14, 2018,
shooting at Marjory Stoneman Douglas (MSD) High School in Parkland,
Florida. Within hours after a gunman killed 17 people at the school, an
angry, outspoken, media-savvy group of student survivors began leading
an effort to change the long-standing dynamic surrounding gun violence.

They gave speeches and interviews, launched a social media campaign using the hashtag #NeverAgain, established a political action committee, and raised millions of dollars in GoFundMe donations. The clearest indication that the Parkland shooting might prove to be a tipping point in the long, contentious debate over gun control took place on March 24, when more than 2 million people joined in a nationwide protest called the March for Our Lives (MFOL). According to the MFOL website, the event was "created by, inspired by, and led by students across the country who will no longer risk their lives waiting for someone else to take action to stop the epidemic of mass school shootings that has become all too familiar" (Rodriguez 2018).

In analyzing how gun control gained traction after the Parkland shooting, some observers noted that the student activists succeeded in mobilizing the so-called mass shooting generation—young people who grew up in the post-Columbine era, with school lockdowns and active-shooter drills making gun violence seem like a basic reality of their existence. "School shootings, and mass shootings in general, have been a part of their lives since they were born, unfortunately," said political science professor Greg Shufeldt. "When tragedy strikes their community, the young survivors are ready to take action. . . . Their reaction is not to grieve silently, for the most part, but to take action and to try and enact change—something no one has been able to do" (S. Miller 2018). Mackenzie Casey, a survivor of the 2012 Sandy Hook school shooting, suggested that the Parkland activists came along at the right time. "This wasn't in our power when it happened to us," she said of the nationwide protests organized by the MSD students. "At this point, almost everyone in the entire country knows someone who has been affected by gun violence, if they haven't been themselves" (Petrusich 2018). Seeing the massive turnout for the MFOL, some commentators compared the Never Again movement to historic youth-led efforts to promote social change, such as the civil rights movement and the Vietnam-era antiwar movement.

Planning the March

The Parkland activists credit the original idea for the MFOL to junior Cameron Kasky, a member of the MSD drama club who began expressing his outrage on social media in the hours after the shooting. He encouraged his friends to use the hashtag #NeverAgain and hosted student meetings at his house to develop a strategy for launching a national gun violence prevention movement. Survivor Jaclyn Corin, the junior class president at MSD, recalled Kasky saying that he wanted to "create a march and get in the media and pull the focus onto the politicians who are performing poorly in their jobs" (L. Miller 2018). The students attributed lawmakers' failure to pass meaningful gun reform legislation to the powerful political influence wielded by the National Rifle Association (NRA) and other gun rights organizations. They argued that by resisting reasonable gun control measures, the NRA and elected officials who accepted NRA money contributed to the prevalence of mass shootings.

The Parkland group quickly expanded to include about 20 MSD survivors, including Emma González, David Hogg, and Delaney Tarr. According to Corin, each student activist took on a different role. "David focuses on the hard facts. Cameron is sarcastic and witty. Emma's strong. I'm more of an organizer," she explained (L. Miller 2018). The students formed a political action committee, Never Again MSD, and devised a plan to maximize the media attention devoted to their cause. They also worked to resolve personal differences of opinion so they could present a unified front. The young activists even discussed specific words they should try to use or avoid using in order to help their message appeal to the widest possible audience. "Literally, we all sat together in a circle and we wrote down on a piece of paper 'no-nos' and 'buzzwords,'" Tarr recalled, "and we were like, 'Okay, so what about this word? Can we say this word?'" (L. Miller 2018).

On February 18, the Never Again activists announced plans for the March for Our Lives, a student-led nationwide demonstration against gun violence to be held on March 24. The primary march was scheduled to take place in Washington, D.C. Supporters who were unable to attend the main march were encouraged to hold sibling protests in cities and towns across the United States. As word spread in the news and on social media, the MFOL registered demonstrations in nearly 800 locations, including in all 50 states and in 90 percent of congressional voting districts nationwide. More than 100 additional marches were planned outside of the United States, on every continent except Antarctica (Sit 2018).

To finance such a major undertaking, the Never Again activists set up an online fund-raiser on the GoFundMe website with a goal of collecting $1 million. To their amazement, they surpassed that ambitious goal in a matter of days, yet donations large and small continued to pour in from across the United States. Celebrities George and Amal Clooney gave the MFOL $500,000, and several other prominent figures in entertainment quickly matched that amount, including Oprah Winfrey and Steven Spielberg. The students eventually ended up with $3.5 million, enough to cover the expenses of the Washington march, assist the organizers of satellite marches, and establish a fund to support the families of victims of the Parkland shooting.

Since the MFOL was inspired by a school shooting, the student organizers decided to make it a youth-led protest. Only young people were allowed to submit poster designs for the event or invited to speak at the Washington protest. As the scope of the MFOL expanded, however, the Parkland teens grew overwhelmed and sought adult assistance. They worked with Everytown for Gun Safety and organizers of the Women's March to obtain permits and arrange logistics, for instance, and they consulted with public relations specialists. "Like, we're organized to a degree, but we're also teenagers, so we're not that organized," Tarr acknowledged (L. Miller 2018).

The Parkland survivors developed a list of legislative goals for the MFOL protest that included digitizing records of gun sales maintained by the Bureau of Alcohol, Tobacco, Firearms, and Explosives; requiring universal background checks for firearm purchases; authorizing the Centers for Disease Control and Prevention to conduct research into the effects of gun violence; limiting the sale of high-capacity ammunition magazines; and banning the sale of assault weapons. According to the MFOL mission statement, "School safety is not a political issue. . . . There cannot be two sides to doing everything in our power to ensure the lives and futures of children who are at risk of dying when they should be learning, playing, and growing. The mission and focus of March for Our Lives is to demand that a comprehensive and effective bill be immediately brought before Congress to address these gun issues" (Gabbatt 2018).

Marching against Gun Violence

Organizers estimated that 800,000 protesters attended the MFOL in Washington, D.C. (Sit 2018), while around 1.7 million more participated in satellite marches in communities across the United States and around the world. Over the course of the day, protesters at the hundreds of marches across the country sent 3.3 million tweets about their experiences (Allen 2018). The main event in the nation's capital attracted a wide range of celebrities, some of whom entertained the crowd with live performances, including Miley Cyrus, Lady Gaga, Selena Gomez, Ariana Grande, Demi Lovato, Lin-Manuel Miranda, and Ben Platt. MSD choir and drama students performed an original song, "Shine"; Andra Day teamed up with rapper Common to perform "Stand Up for Something"; and Jennifer Hudson sang Bob Dylan's classic protest song "The Times They Are A-Changin'," with backing vocals by the D.C. Choir.

The Washington march also featured speeches by 20 student activists, including 10 Parkland survivors as well as young people from other communities whose lives had been affected by school shootings or other gun violence. Tarr warned members of Congress that the young protesters would not be satisfied with token changes to the nation's gun laws and planned to continue fighting until they achieved meaningful reform. "We are not here for bread crumbs; we are here for real change," she declared. "We are here to lead, we are here to call out every single politician to force them into enacting this legislation" (Shabad, Bailey, and McCausland 2018). "We hereby promise to fix the broken system we've been forced into and create a better world for the generations to come," Kasky added. "Don't worry, we've got this" (Shabad, Bailey, and McCausland 2018).

Corin used the platform granted to MSD survivors to advocate for children from poor and minority communities, noting that they faced much higher statistical risks of becoming victims of gun violence. "We recognize that Parkland received more attention because of its affluence," she stated. "But we share this stage today and forever with those communities who have always stared down the barrel of a gun" (Shabad, Bailey, and McCausland 2018). Corin introduced Yolanda Renee King, the nine-year-old granddaughter of slain civil rights leader Martin Luther King Jr. "My grandfather had a dream that his four children would not be judged by the color of their skin but by the content of their character," she said. "I have a dream that enough is enough and that this should be a gun-free world. Period" (Shabad, Bailey, and McCausland 2018).

Naomi Wadler, a fifth-grade student who organized a walkout protest at her elementary school in Alexandria, Virginia, also delivered a speech. "I represent the African-American women who are victims of gun violence, who are simply statistics instead of vibrant, beautiful girls full of potential," she declared. "My friends and I might still be 11, and we might still be in elementary school, but we know. We know life isn't equal for everyone and we know what is right and wrong. We also know that we stand in the shadow of the Capitol, and we know that we have seven short years until we too have the right to vote" (Amatulli 2018). Other speakers included Edna Lisbeth Chavez, a 17-year-old activist from South Los Angeles who lost her brother Ricardo to gun violence; 17-year-old Zion Kelly, whose twin brother, Zaire, was shot and killed while walking home from school in Washington, D.C.; and 9-year-old Christopher Underwood of Brooklyn, New York, who became a gun control advocate after his 14-year-old brother Akeal was shot and killed on a street corner.

González delivered the last speech at the Washington march. After naming the victims of the MSD shooting and mentioning things they would never again experience, she stopped speaking and stood silently with tears streaming down her face for several minutes. Finally, she announced that she had been onstage for 6 minutes and 20 seconds—the same amount of time it took the perpetrator of the MSD school shooting to murder 17 of her classmates and teachers. "The shooter has ceased shooting, and will soon abandon his rifle, blend in with the students as they escape, and walk free for an hour before arrest," she said. "Fight for your lives before it's someone else's job" (Shabad, Bailey, and McCausland 2018).

Responses to the MFOL varied depending on the observer's political leanings. The Parkland student organizers and their allies received effusive praise from many liberals and Democrats. Some supporters compared the march to the huge student-led protests against the Vietnam War and racial segregation policies during the 1960s and 1970s. Many predicted that the demonstrations would force political leaders to take action and address the students' demands for stricter gun laws. Many conservatives and Republicans, on the other hand, dismissed the MFOL as insignificant and said that the student protesters were too young to fully understand complex political issues. Some opponents claimed that the Parkland organizers were being financed and manipulated by powerful adults to promote a liberal agenda and destroy Second Amendment rights. "In our system, inalienable rights—including the one to self-defense—can't be swept away by angry crowds," said *Federalist* editor David Harsanyi. "Yet we live with the insufferable need to act as if protesting is tantamount to patriotism rather than a collective act of frustration" (Cummings 2018).

A significant goal of the MFOL involved registering young voters and encouraging them to use their collective power to remove politicians from office who accepted campaign contributions from the NRA. In a CNN town hall discussion, the Parkland activists pointed out that Republican senator Marco Rubio of Florida had received $3.3 million from the NRA throughout his political career. The students asked Rubio to reject NRA funding in the future, but he refused, arguing that many of his constituents supported the Second Amendment. In response, many student protesters at the Washington march wore orange price tags that read "$1.05," which they claimed was the monetary value Rubio placed on the life of each of the 3.1 million school-age young people in Florida. The activists vowed to support candidates who favored meaningful reform of the nation's gun laws until their generation reached an age when they could assume leadership of the country.

Further Reading

Allen, Mike. 2018. "Yesterday's Global Roar for Gun Control." Axios, March 25, 2018. https://www.axios.com/march-for-our-lives-on-the-ground-penn sylvania-avenue-81881f02-8c51-4367-9379-ed1760cbe441.html.

Amatulli, Jenna. 2018. "11-Year-Old Activist Honors Black Girls Whose Stories Never Make the News." Huffington Post, March 24, 2018. https://www .huffingtonpost.com/entry/naomi-wadler-march-for-our-lives_us_5ab68 cdbe4b054d118e3548a.

Corin, Jaclyn. 2018. "I Helped Organize the March for Our Lives Because There Is Strength in Numbers." *Seventeen,* March 21, 2018. https://www.seven-teen.com/life/real-girl-stories/a19480107/jaclyn-corin-march-for-our -lives-protest-gun-control/.

Cummings, William. 2018. "The Bubble: March for Our Lives Protesters Dis-missed by Conservatives." *USA Today,* March 26, 2018. https://www .usatoday.com/story/news/politics/onpolitics/2018/03/26/media-reac tions-march-our-lives/460029002/.

Gabbatt, Adam. 2018. "Hopes for Half a Million to March for 'Commonsense' Gun Solutions." *The Guardian,* February 24, 2018. https://www.theguard ian.com/us-news/2018/feb/24/the-resistance-now-march-washington -gun-solutions.

March for Our Lives. 2018. https://marchforourlives.com/.

Miller, Lisa. 2018. "War Room." New York Magazine, March 5, 2018. http:// nymag.com/intelligencer/2018/03/on-the-ground-with-parkland-teens -as-they-plot-a-revolution.html?gtm=bottom&gtm=bottom.

Miller, Susan. 2018. "'We Will Be the Last Mass Shooting': Florida Students Want to Be Tipping Point in Gun Debate." *USA Today,* February 17, 2018. https://www.usatoday.com/story/news/nation/2018/02/17/we-last -mass-shooting-florida-students-might-tipping-point-gun-debate/34799 2002/.

Petrusich, Amanda. 2018. "The Fearless, Outraged Young Protesters at the March for Our Lives." *New Yorker,* March 24, 2018. https://www.newyorker .com/news/news-desk/the-march-for-our-lives-photographs-from -washington-dc.

Rodriguez, Victoria. 2018. "Students and Teachers Explain Why They're Joining 'March for Our Lives.'" *Seventeen,* March 2, 2018. https://www.seventeen .com/life/school/a18375585/students-teachers-march-for-our-lives/.

Shabad, Rebecca, Chelsea Bailey, and Phil McCausland. 2018. "At March for Our Lives, Survivors Lead Hundreds of Thousands in Call for Change." NBC News, March 24, 2018. https://www.nbcnews.com/news/us-news/march -our-lives-draws-hundreds-thousands-washington-around-nation-n85 9716.

Sit, Ryan. 2018. "More Than 2 Million in 90 Percent of Voting Districts Joined March for Our Lives Protests." *Newsweek,* March 26, 2018. https://www

.newsweek.com/march-our-lives-how-many-2-million-90-voting-district
-860841.

Smiley, David, and Alex Daugherty. 2018. "Parkland Students Have a Cause and
$3.5 Million. Here's How They're Going to Spend It." *Miami Herald,* February 21, 2018. https://www.miamiherald.com/news/local/community
/broward/article201464304.html#storylink=cpy.

The Santa Fe High School Shooting (2018)

Less than two months after the March for Our Lives mobilized students across the United States to demand legislative action to prevent school shootings, another mass shooting occurred at Santa Fe High School in Santa Fe, Texas. On May 18, 2018, a 17-year-old student armed with a shotgun and a .38-caliber revolver murdered 10 people and wounded 13 others before surrendering to an armed school resource officer. The incident marked the 16th U.S. school shooting of 2018 and prompted thousands of students to share their thoughts, fears, and last wishes on social media using the hashtag #IfIShouldDieInASchoolShooting (Martin et al. 2018).

The Incident

Santa Fe High School serves around 1,400 students in a community located between Houston and Galveston in southeastern Texas. At 7:40 a.m. on May 18, junior Dimitrios Pagourtzis reportedly entered a cluster of four art classrooms, pulled two guns from beneath a trench coat, exclaimed "Surprise," and began shooting. Upon hearing the sounds of gunfire, many students hid in supply closets or ran to escape from the school. Two armed school resource officers arrived on the scene within a few minutes and engaged the shooter. Both the gunman and one of the officers sustained gunshot wounds. The other officer then negotiated the perpetrator's surrender and took him into custody.

The Santa Fe school shooting claimed the lives of two teachers and eight students, including an international exchange student who was scheduled to return home to Pakistan a week later. Police later found evidence suggesting that the gunman had planned his actions to emulate the perpetrators of the 1999 shooting at Columbine High School in Littleton, Colorado. He wore similar clothing, placed explosive devices in and around the school, and originally intended to commit suicide. "It's a form of celebrity worship," said criminology professor Adam Lankford. "The celebrities in this case are celebrity killers—the Columbine killers" (Martin et al. 2018).

Unlike the perpetrators of the Columbine shooting, the Santa Fe shooter provided few clues about his violent intentions. He was known as an introvert and a loner, but he received good grades in school and played on the junior varsity football team. Some classmates claimed that he had been the victim of bullying, but others disputed that assertion. The parents of a female student who was killed said the gunman had stalked and threatened her in the weeks prior to her death. Once in custody, the perpetrator confessed to the shooting and said he used guns that his father legally purchased. Although it remained unclear whether the shooter had targeted specific students, he told police that he had spared the lives of students he liked.

The Aftermath

Reactions to the Santa Fe High School shooting mirrored those that followed earlier school shootings. Students, parents, political leaders, and law enforcement officers expressed grief and anger and debated about whether and how the tragedy could have been prevented. Notably, however, few members of the mass shooting generation seemed surprised that the incident occurred. According to the *Washington Post,* at least 141 children and educators were killed and 284 others wounded in school shootings since Columbine (Martin et al. 2018). Santa Fe student Paige Curry, who hid backstage in the auditorium with other students during the shooting, told a reporter that she expected gun violence to affect her school at some point. "It's been happening everywhere," she stated. "I always felt like eventually it would happen here. I wasn't surprised; I was just scared" (Fernandez 2018). Many media outlets aired her response, which also went viral online. Gun control advocates contended that Curry's attitude demonstrated the heartbreaking reality that America's young people had come to view themselves as potential targets of school shootings. Across the country, thousands of students shared their feelings of vulnerability by using the hashtag #IfIShouldDieInASchoolShooting on social media.

The student survivors of the February 2018 shooting at Marjory Stoneman Douglas (MSD) High School in Florida, who launched the Never Again movement and organized the March for Our Lives, expressed their condolences and support to the Santa Fe students and families. "This is not the price of our freedom," they posted on Twitter. "This is the most fatal shooting since the one at our school and tragedies like this will continue to happen unless action is taken." MSD student Ryan Deitsch added, "Politics aside, how many more have to die before we can change?" Some of the Never Again activists criticized the response of President Donald Trump, who tweeted "School shooting in Texas. Early reports not looking good. God bless all!" March for Our Lives organizer Jaclyn Corin replied, "Our children are being MURDERED and you're treating this like a game. . . . DO SOMETHING" (Lang 2018).

In Texas, many state and local officials expressed determination to take action to prevent gun violence. Houston police chief Art Avecedo challenged Second Amendment supporters who argued that stricter gun laws would not help solve the problem of school shootings. "I know some have strong feelings about gun rights, but I want you to know I've hit rock bottom and I am not interested in your views as it pertains to this issue," he declared. "It's a time for prayers, action, and the asking of God's forgiveness for our inaction (especially the elected officials that ran to the cameras today, acted in a solemn manner, called for prayers, and will once again do absolutely nothing)" (Hanna et al. 2018). Texas Republican governor Greg Abbott submitted a proposed plan of action to the state legislature. He recommended adopting new state laws to require citizens to report the loss or theft of firearms, strengthen background checks for gun purchases, and institute red flag provisions to prevent dangerous people from owning guns. "We need to do more than just pray for the victims and their families," he stated. "It's in Texas that we take action, to step up and make sure this tragedy is never repeated" (Chappell and Romo 2018).

As was the case with previous school shootings, however, the Santa Fe tragedy did not produce legislative action at either the federal or state level. The Texas legislature refused to consider Abbott's proposals and instead focused on measures aimed at improving school security and increasing access to mental health services for troubled students. School district officials in Santa Fe implemented several changes intended to increase student safety, such as hiring additional resource officers, installing metal detectors at building entrances, placing panic buttons in every classroom, strengthening antibullying policies, and monitoring student social media accounts for evidence of violent intentions (Jervis 2018).

Further Reading

Chappell, Bill, and Vanessa Romo. 2018. "Ten People Killed in Texas High School Shooting; Suspect in Custody." *National Public Radio*, May 18, 2018. https://www.npr.org/sections/thetwo-way/2018/05/18/612286146/shooting-reported-at-high-school-near-houston.

Fernandez, Manny, Richard Fausset, and Jess Bidgood. 2018. "In Texas School Shooting, Ten Dead, Ten Hurt, and Many Unsurprised." *New York Times*,

May 18, 2018. https://www.nytimes.com/2018/05/18/us/school-shooting
-santa-fe-texas.html.

Hanna, Jason, Dakin Andone, Keith Allen, and Steve Almasy. 2018. "Alleged
Shooter at Texas High School Spared People He Liked, Court Document
Says." CNN, May 18, 2018. https://www.cnn.com/2018/05/18/us/texas
-school-shooting/index.html.

Jervis, Rick. 2018. "Santa Fe High Students Return to Site of Deadly Texas Shooting with More Security." *USA Today,* August 20, 2018. https://www.usato
day.com/story/news/2018/08/20/santa-fe-high-texas-school-shooting
-back-school/1030660002/.

Lang, Marissa J. 2018. "Here's What Parkland Survivors Are Saying about the
Santa Fe School Shooting." *Washington Post,* May 18, 2018. https://www
.washingtonpost.com/news/education/wp/2018/05/18/heres-what-park
land-survivors-are-saying-about-the-santa-fe-school-shooting/?utm
_term=.2c49303d17e2.

Martin, Brittney, Mark Berman, Joel Achenbach, and Amy B. Wang. 2018. "'Overwhelming Grief': Eight Students, Two Teachers Killed in Texas High
School Shooting." *Washington Post,* May 20, 2018. https://www.washing
tonpost.com/news/post-nation/wp/2018/05/19/ten-killed-in-texas-high
-school-shooting-were-mostly-students-police-say-suspect-confessed
/?utm_term=.5175bea5823d.

CHAPTER THREE

Impacts of the Never Again Movement

This chapter examines the impact of the Never Again movement on specific areas of American life and culture. It reviews the status of the demands presented by student activists at the March for Our Lives, explores the controversy surrounding proposals to increase school security and arm teachers, and analyzes whether the wave of youth activism precipitated by the Parkland survivors can shift the national debate about gun violence prevention.

The March for Our Lives Demands

When they launched the Never Again movement and organized the March for Our Lives, the student activists from Marjory Stoneman Douglas (MSD) High School in Parkland, Florida, established a list of legislative demands. They originally sought five specific changes to the nation's gun laws aimed at reducing the prevalence of gun violence and preventing future school shootings. "As a nation, we continue to witness tragedy after tragedy, yet our politicians remain complacent," read the mission statement on the March for Our Lives website. "The Parkland students, along with young leaders of all backgrounds from across the country, refuse to accept this passivity and demand direct action to combat this epidemic."

The list of demands eventually expanded to include 10 items, ranging from some that enjoy broad public support and are considered politically achievable in the short term to some that are viewed as highly controversial and unlikely to occur without a long-term cultural shift. The following sections examine the current status and future outlook of the demands as of fall 2018—six months after the March for Our Lives brought gun control to the forefront of the national consciousness.

Demand #1: Restore CDC Funding for Gun Violence Research

In 1996, Republican representative Jay Dickey of Arkansas introduced a rider to an appropriations bill that read "none of the funds made available for injury prevention and control" in the budget of the U.S. Centers for Disease Control and Prevention (CDC) could be used to "advocate or promote gun control" (Mosher and Gould 2018). Known as the Dickey Amendment, this measure effectively prohibited the CDC from conducting scientific research into the effects of gun violence as a public health issue. Congress also reduced the CDC budget by $2.6 million, which corresponded to the amount the agency dedicated to gun violence research the previous year.

Gun violence is a leading cause of death in the United States, affecting 1 out of every 315 people. For an average American, the chance of dying from gun violence is 10 times higher than the chance of dying in an earthquake, a tornado, a hurricane, a flood, or another force of nature (Mosher and Gould 2018). Although diseases, injuries, accidents, and other public health risks receive extensive government-funded study aimed at preventing untimely deaths, the Dickey Amendment restricts the CDC from examining the health implications of gun ownership. As a result, gun violence was the least researched among the 30 top causes of death in the United States from 2004 to 2015. Although guns killed as many people as sepsis each year, gun violence research received only 0.7 percent as much funding (Stark and Shah 2017).

Gun control advocates have long argued that the Dickey Amendment, by preventing the collection of objective data on the health effects of gun violence, makes it difficult for lawmakers to evaluate the problem and develop effective policies to reduce gun-related deaths. They point out that research by private institutions has found connections between the widespread availability and ownership of guns and high rates of gun violence. In 2016, a coalition of 141 medical organizations representing more than 1 million health care providers issued a statement calling for repeal of the Dickey Amendment. They argued that scientific studies could reveal valuable information that would help reduce firearm accidents and suicides. "The medical and public health communities continue to believe gun violence, which claims an average of 91 American lives daily, is a serious public health threat that must be handled with urgency," said

Alice Chen of Doctors for America. "Congress must lift the barrier to research that has persisted for nearly 20 years and fund the work that we need to save lives and prevent future tragedies" (McCarthy 2016).

Dickey, who left Congress in 2001, told an interviewer that he never intended to stop the CDC from conducting research on gun violence. Rather, he hoped that the amendment would prevent the agency from politicizing study results by advocating for gun control policies. He argued that preventing gun-related deaths did not necessarily mean restricting the gun ownership rights of law-abiding citizens. "The highway industry spent money in their scientific research to figure out what could be done [to reduce fatal accidents], assuming that they were going to allow cars to continue to be on our highways," he explained. "We could do the same in the gun industry. . . . And I think it's a shame that we haven't" (Inskeep 2015).

The National Rifle Association (NRA) and other gun rights organizations consistently used their political influence to oppose efforts to repeal the Dickey Amendment and restore CDC funding. In 2011, Second Amendment supporters convinced their allies in Congress to add a similar restriction to the budget of the National Institutes of Health. Following the 2012 mass shooting at Sandy Hook Elementary School in Newtown, Connecticut, President Barack Obama issued a memorandum instructing the CDC to resume studying the causes of gun violence. Congress rejected Obama's requests to fund the research, however, so the directive produced few results.

In the wake of the MSD school shooting, the Parkland student activists included repeal of the Dickey Amendment on their list of legislative demands. Restoring CDC funding for gun violence research became a priority of the Never Again movement, raising public awareness of the issue and generating pressure on Congress to take action. Some lawmakers viewed gun violence research as a relatively painless step toward placating gun control activists. Officials in the Donald Trump administration, such as Secretary of Health and Human Services Alex Azar, downplayed the significance of the Dickey Amendment, claiming that it did not expressly forbid the CDC from conducting gun violence research, but only prohibited the agency from advocating for specific policies.

In March 2018, Congress included a provision in its budget bill that clarified the purpose of the Dickey Amendment and weakened restrictions on federal gun violence research. Under the new legislation, the CDC obtained explicit permission to investigate the causes of gun violence, although it was still prohibited from "using appropriated funding to advocate or promote gun control" (Bryan 2018). Although the Parkland students and other gun control advocates supported the change, they asserted that it would not lead to an increase in gun violence research unless Congress also approved additional funding for the CDC.

Demand #2: Enable the ATF to Digitize Gun Registration Data

The Bureau of Alcohol, Tobacco, Firearms, and Explosives (ATF) is the federal agency charged with regulating the U.S. gun industry. Since the Gun Control Act of 1968 created the ATF, the NRA and other gun rights organizations have sought to limit its power and curtail its enforcement activities. These efforts resulted in the passage of the Firearms Owners' Protection Act (FOPA) of 1986, which established limits on ATF inspections of gun dealers and prohibited the federal government from compiling a national registry of gun ownership from dealer records. Congress also barred the ATF from "consolidation or centralization" of gun dealers' records into a searchable electronic database.

Gun rights proponents argue that laws requiring federal registration and licensing of firearms or allowing compilation of digital gun ownership records violate individuals' rights under the Second Amendment. NRA leaders claim that if the federal government maintained an electronic database of gun sales, the information could be used to confiscate guns from private citizens. "We support enforcement of the laws on the books and ATF efforts to apprehend and prosecute violent criminals," said NRA spokesperson Jennifer Baker. "We have and will continue to oppose political appointees looking to enact an anti-gun agenda through the regulatory process, making it more difficult for law-abiding citizens to exercise their constitutional rights while criminals continue to break the law" (Watkins 2018).

Gun control advocates contend that the restrictions on ATF record keeping make it difficult for the agency to perform its mandated functions, such as providing information to help law enforcement solve gun-related crimes. The ATF operates the National Tracing Center, which houses 800 million records of gun sales by dealers that are no longer in business. When the ATF receives a request from law enforcement to trace the source of a gun used to commit a crime, agents must search manually through thousands of records. The agency received more than 373,000 such requests in 2015, and processing each request took an average of four to seven business days. "Congress imposes conflicting directives on the ATF," wrote Dan Friedman in a Trace article. "The agency is required to trace guns, but it must use inefficient procedures and obsolete technology. Lawmakers in effect tell the agency to do a job, but badly" (Friedman

2016). The Tiahrt Amendment—introduced by Republican representative Todd Tiahrt of Kansas in 2003—prohibits the National Tracing Center from releasing gun trace data except for the specific records requested by law enforcement. This provision prevents the use of firearms tracing information in gun violence research and civil lawsuits against gun manufacturers.

After the MSD school shooting, the Parkland survivors drew attention to the limitations placed on the ATF, which they claimed made it impossible for the agency to maintain effective oversight of the gun industry. The list of demands for the March for Our Lives included changing federal law to allow the ATF to digitize its records and create a searchable database of gun sales. Never Again activists noted that government registration and licensing requirements already applied to automobiles, boats, and even pets without infringing on individual rights and freedoms. They argued that creating a modern, computerized, searchable database would enable the ATF to instantly trace the sales history of guns used in crimes, providing vital information to help law enforcement speed up criminal investigations and save lives.

In response to the concerns expressed by March for Our Lives activists, Democratic senators Patrick Leahy of Vermont and Bill Nelson of Florida introduced the Crime Gun Tracing Modernization Act in May 2018. The sponsors described the measure as bringing the ATF into the twenty-first century by allowing the agency to digitize its records and consolidate them in a searchable computer database. "Relenting to pressure from the gun lobby, Congress placed archaic hurdles on crime gun traces, prohibiting the ATF from digitizing or electronically searching through firearms records," Leahy stated. "This bill is a commonsense crime-fighting reform to end this antiquated and nonsensical restriction. It would permit electronic searches of records that ATF already has access to but cannot quickly search due to absurd hurdles in the law" (Leahy 2018). The legislation was referred to the Senate Judiciary Committee but appeared unlikely to go further.

Demand #3: Institute Universal Background Checks on Gun Purchases

The Brady Handgun Violence Prevention Act of 1993 required federally licensed gun dealers to conduct criminal background checks on individual firearm purchasers. It also authorized creation of the National Instant Criminal Background Check System (NICS), maintained by the Federal Bureau of Investigation, to enable these checks to be completed quickly and accurately. When a gun dealer submits the name of a prospective buyer to the federal NICS database, it is checked against criminal and mental health records provided by state and federal courts and law enforcement agencies. According to Everytown for Gun Safety, between 1994 and 2016 the federal background check system blocked 3 million attempted gun purchases by individuals who were prohibited from owning firearms under federal law, such as convicted felons, fugitives from justice, domestic abusers, people dishonorably discharged from the military, people residing in the United States unlawfully, and people with documented drug addiction or mental illness.

Following the MSD school shooting, the student activists who launched the Never Again movement drew attention to what they viewed as a significant limitation in the federal background check system: the Brady Bill did not require background checks for guns purchased from private, unlicensed sellers. They argued that this "private sale loophole" made it easy for dangerous people to buy firearms online, at gun shows, or even at garage sales without having to undergo a criminal background check. Everytown for Gun Safety estimated that 22 percent of gun transfers nationwide were conducted without a background check, and that 10 percent of people who purchased guns from unlicensed sellers were legally prohibited from owning firearms ("The Background Check Loophole" 2018). March for Our Lives organizers demanded that Congress pass legislation to close the loophole and require universal background checks on all gun purchases.

NRA lobbyists opposed universal background checks, arguing that private individuals should be allowed to buy, sell, or trade firearms among themselves without government interference. They claimed that such restrictions would be difficult to enforce, causing law enforcement agencies to spend valuable time and resources trying to track down illegal gun transfers rather than fighting more serious crimes. They also asserted that universal background checks would not reduce gun violence, noting that most perpetrators of mass shootings used guns that they obtained legally after undergoing background checks.

NRA leaders instead proposed making the existing NICS database more comprehensive by improving the flow of information from state and federal agencies. They contended that background checks were ineffective because of lapses in reporting the names of people convicted of criminal offenses or deemed mentally ill. The mass shooter who killed 26 people at a Texas church in 2017, for instance, had been discharged from the military for domestic abuse, yet he passed a background test because the Department of Defense failed to report that information to the NICS. In the aftermath of the MSD shooting, Congress passed the Fix NICS Act of

2017. President Donald Trump signed it into law on March 23, 2018—one day before an estimated 2 million people nationwide took part in the March for Our Lives protests. The law established both incentives and penalties designed to increase the amount and accuracy of information reported to the background check system.

Although Never Again supporters applauded the passage of the Fix NICS Act, they considered it a modest first step toward preventing dangerous people from purchasing firearms and continued to push for universal background checks. In an effort to close the federal loophole, 20 states and the District of Columbia enacted their own laws requiring background checks for at least some private gun purchases. Some states required private gun sales to be processed through licensed dealers or law enforcement agencies, while others required all gun buyers to pass a background check to obtain a state permit. Proponents of universal background checks claimed that these states saw reductions in gun violence, including firearm suicides, law enforcement personnel killed on duty, and women killed by domestic partners. In addition, they noted that universal background checks received widespread public support. A Quinnipiac University survey conducted one week after the Parkland shooting found that 97 percent of American voters—including those who live in gun-owning households—supported requiring all gun buyers to undergo background checks ("U.S. Support for Gun Control" 2018).

Demand #4: Eliminate Large-Capacity Ammunition Magazines

Another legislative demand issued by the March for Our Lives organizers involves reinstating a federal ban on large-capacity magazines (LCMs), which are generally defined as those capable of holding more than 10 rounds of ammunition. Gun control advocates argue that LCMs increase the death toll in mass shootings by allowing perpetrators to fire up to 100 rounds in rapid succession without stopping to reload. They assert that the need to reload forces mass shooters to pause momentarily, enabling law enforcement to intervene or potential victims to escape. "Even though it's fairly easy to interchange magazines, any time you do is a point at which firing stops," said gun policy expert Robert Spitzer. "People drop the magazines. They jam. In a real live fire situation, people are often nervous, even including those who are committing these crimes" (Wing 2018). After firing nearly 150 rounds in six minutes, the MSD school shooter experienced a problem while reloading that convinced him to drop his weapon and leave the scene.

Never Again activists cite studies showing that LCMs were used in half of the 62 mass shootings that occurred between 1982 and 2012, and that these incidents resulted in 57 percent more deaths and 135 percent more nonfatal gunshot wounds than mass shootings that involved magazines of 10 rounds or less (Freskos 2018). LCMs played a role in all of the deadliest U.S. school shootings, including those at Columbine High School (1999), Sandy Hook Elementary School (2012), and MSD High School. In the deadliest mass shooting in U.S. history, the perpetrator used semiautomatic weapons equipped with 100-round magazines to kill 58 people and wound 400 others at an outdoor music festival in Las Vegas, Nevada, in 2017.

Large-capacity ammunition magazines did not gain popularity until the 1980s, when the U.S. gun industry shifted toward marketing and production of semiautomatic handguns capable of accepting detachable magazines. The Violent Crime Control and Law Enforcement Act of 1994 prohibited the manufacture and sale of semiautomatic assault weapons as well as any "large capacity ammunition feeding device" with a capacity of more than 10 rounds of ammunition. The law did not apply to LCMs that were manufactured and sold before the ban took effect, however, so many remained in circulation. Under pressure from the NRA, Congress allowed the federal assault weapons ban to expire in 2004, which made LCMs legal under federal law once again.

Nine states and the District of Columbia enacted their own restrictions on the size of ammunition magazines, and more than a dozen municipalities followed suit. Rather than including grandfather clauses allowing gun owners to retain possession of previously purchased LCMs, several jurisdictions required citizens to sell, turn in, or destroy them once the bans took effect. California voters approved a referendum in 2016 banning the sale or possession of LCMs, but the NRA filed a lawsuit to block implementation of the law. In November 2018, a mass shooter used a semiautomatic handgun equipped with an LCM to kill 12 people at a country music bar in Thousand Oaks, California. Gun control advocates argued that without NRA interference, the law could have prevented the shooter from gaining access to a banned LCM. "We refuse to take the blame that is commonly misplaced on those of us who simply wish to protect ourselves, our families, or to shoot for sport," the gun rights group responsible for the lawsuit said in a statement. "We do not know what was going on in the mind of the terrorist who took the lives of the innocent victims in Thousand Oaks last night. But we do know one thing for sure: punishing the rest of us isn't the answer" (Axelrod 2018).

Gun rights supporters list many objections to reinstating the federal ban on LCMs. For instance, they note that tens of millions of LCMs are already in circulation, so a ban would have little impact on their availability. In addition, they argue that many modern firearms are built to accept magazines larger than 10 rounds, making LCMs a form of standard equipment rather than an optional accessory. Critics also claim that banning LCMs would not reduce mass shootings or increase public safety because perpetrators can cause the same amount of damage by carrying multiple 10-round magazines and reloading quickly. Finally, NRA lobbyists argue that arbitrarily banning certain types of ammunition infringes upon the Second Amendment rights of gun owners and compromises their ability to defend themselves. These arguments appeared to be losing traction with the public, however, as 70 percent of respondents in a February 2018 Politico/Morning Consult poll expressed support for a federal ban on LCMs (Shepard 2018).

Demand #5: Ban Military-Style Assault Weapons

The gunman who killed 17 people at MSD High School, like the perpetrators of many of the deadliest U.S. mass shootings, used an AR-15–style semiautomatic rifle. Semiautomatic firearms—which can take the form of rifles, handguns, or shotguns—fire a single round each time the user pulls the trigger, then automatically reload the chamber and reset the firing mechanism. Military-style semiautomatic rifles usually accept a detachable ammunition magazine and have additional features that enable users to fire quickly and accurately. Gun control advocates refer to these high-powered, military-style firearms as "assault rifles" and "weapons of war," while gun rights supporters prefer the term "modern sporting rifles."

March for Our Lives organizers demanded a federal ban on the manufacture, sale, or possession of assault weapons by civilians. They contend that these weapons—which closely resemble the firearms regularly issued to U.S. infantry troops—are not necessary for normal civilian uses such as hunting and self-defense. "They are the Formula One cars of guns, designed to kill as many people as quickly and efficiently as possible," said U.S. Marine Corps combat veteran Joe Plenzler, leader of a veterans' group that supports an assault weapons ban. "We are seeing battlefield-level casualties because we are allowing those weapons on our street" (Chivers et al. 2018).

The federal government banned assault weapons for a decade under the Violent Crime Control and Law Enforcement Act, which President Bill Clinton signed into law in 1994. The law prohibited the manufacture and sale of 19 specific military-style rifles—such as the AR-15, AK-47, and Uzi—as well as other semiautomatic firearms with detachable magazines and certain other features, including pistol grips, folding or telescoping stocks, and flash suppressors. The law also banned the sale of large-capacity ammunition magazines, defined as those capable of firing more than 10 rounds in succession. The ban only applied to new weapons, meaning that an estimated 1.5 million previously purchased guns remained in circulation. After Congress allowed the law to expire in 2004, seven states and the District of Columbia passed their own assault weapons bans.

Shortly after the MSD school shooting, Democratic congressman David Cicilline of Rhode Island introduced House Resolution 5087, the assault weapons ban of 2018. The legislation proposed a ban on the sale of new semiautomatic firearms with specific military-style features, including pistol grips, forward grips, threaded barrels, barrel shrouds, and folding, telescoping, or detachable stocks. The bill allowed gun owners to maintain possession of such firearms purchased prior to the ban, although it made all future sales of those weapons subject to federal background checks. The bill also banned ammunition magazines with a capacity larger than 10 rounds. Among the bill's supporters was Democratic senator Mark Warner of Virginia, who had voted against a similar ban in 2013. "The features and tactical accessories that define assault weapons under this legislation were designed for a specific purpose—to give soldiers an advantage over the enemy, not to mow down students in school hallways," he stated. "No American wants criminals, terrorists or dangerously ill teenagers to get their hands on a weapon capable of so much destruction" (Warner 2018).

The assault weapons ban of 2018 faced staunch opposition from the NRA and other gun rights advocates. Opponents of the ban argued that banning assault weapons would not reduce gun violence. They pointed out that assault rifles were used in only 3 percent of gun homicides, whereas handguns were used in 70 percent. They also noted that Americans already owned an estimated 8 million guns that would be defined as "assault weapons" by the proposed law and would remain in circulation under its grandfather provisions (Lopez 2018). Although Never Again activists wanted the ban to apply to assault weapons already in private hands, the NRA claimed that any federal effort to confiscate guns from law-abiding citizens—whether through buyback programs, tax schemes, or mandatory licensing and registration requirements—violated citizens' right to bear arms under the Second Amendment.

Even proponents of an assault weapons ban acknowledge that it would be challenging to enforce. Many gun manufacturers circumvented the 1994 law by making small, cosmetic changes to firearm features and accessories. Some gun control advocates shifted their emphasis away from seeking an assault weapons ban and prioritized other reforms, such as expanded background checks, that faced less opposition and enjoyed more popular support. The March for Our Lives organizers continued to push for the ban, however, arguing that it would significantly reduce the number of lives lost in mass shootings.

Although the Trump administration opposed reinstatement of the federal assault weapons ban, in March 2018 it announced plans to prohibit the sale of bump stocks—accessories that enable semiautomatic weapons to fire continuously with a single pull of the trigger. These attachments effectively make semiautomatic weapons function like fully automatic weapons or machine guns, which have been subject to strict federal regulation since the 1930s. The U.S. Department of Justice described the new restriction as an administrative rule change that placed bump stocks in the same legal category as machine guns. Some observers credited the Republican administration's action, which was announced one day before the March for Our Lives protests, to the growing influence of the Never Again movement. Critics, however, described bump stocks as "novelty items" and said they were used so rarely that banning them would have no effect on gun violence (Burrus 2018).

Demands #6–10: Address the Root Causes of Gun Violence

In the months following the March for Our Lives, Never Again activists added several more items to their original list of legislative demands. These priorities went beyond commonly cited gun control measures to include policies and programs intended to address the root causes of gun violence, especially in the urban areas where it is most prevalent. At the March for Our Lives, the organizers invited students of color from economically disadvantaged backgrounds to provide their perspectives on the gun control debate. Although school shootings in predominantly white, affluent suburbs attracted media attention, the Parkland students recognized that minority children from impoverished urban areas faced a much higher risk of becoming victims of gun violence. According to the CDC, 81 percent of the nearly 13,000 firearm homicides in the United States in 2015 occurred in large cities, and black residents were eight times more likely to be killed than white residents (Pahn, Knopov, and Siegel 2018). As part of their commitment to address gun violence in all its forms, the Never Again activists called for increased state and federal funding for evidence-based intervention programs that have been proven to reduce homicide rates in high-crime urban areas.

March for Our Lives organizers also called on Congress to make gun trafficking a federal offense in order to prevent the illegal flow of firearms from states with weak gun control laws to those with strong gun control laws. They noted that the inconsistencies in state laws and the lack of a clear federal prohibition facilitated illegal transfers of firearms and enabled dangerous criminals to obtain guns. The student activists also expressed support for other antitrafficking measures, including more frequent ATF inspections to crack down on corrupt or irresponsible gun dealers, universal background checks to prevent illegal gun sales by unlicensed private sellers, mandatory reporting for lost or stolen firearms, and digitizing ATF records to expedite crime gun tracing and prevent straw purchases (buying a gun on behalf of another person). The Gun Trafficking Prevention Act, which would institute a federal ban on buying or selling guns with the intent to transfer them illegally, was introduced in Congress in 2013, 2015, and 2017 but failed to generate enough support for passage.

March for Our Lives organizers also expressed support for red flag laws, which are designed to eliminate access to guns by people who pose a risk of harm to themselves or others. Also known as Extreme Risk Protection Orders (ERPO), these legal tools allow concerned family members or law enforcement personnel to petition a court for a warrant to remove firearms from the possession of people in crisis. Grounds for granting an ERPO might include an individual exhibiting warning signs of suicide or threatening to harm another person. The individual is afforded due process protections and allowed to present evidence in court. If an ERPO is granted, the individual is temporarily prohibited from possessing or purchasing firearms, usually for a period of one year. Advocates argued that red flag laws had the potential to reduce gun violence, especially since firearm suicides account for two-thirds of all gun-related deaths in the United States (Burrus 2018). Whereas five states had red flag laws in place prior to 2018, eight more states—including Florida—passed such measures in the months after the MSD school shooting.

Never Again activists also called for stricter laws to prevent domestic abusers from gaining access to firearms. They pointed to studies showing that firearm violence by an intimate partner is responsible for more than half of all murders of women in the United States. Although federal law prohibits people convicted of domestic violence or subject to a domestic violence restraining order from purchasing or possessing guns, it does not mandate a process for domestic abusers to surrender any guns they own. As a result, many domestic abusers take advantage of more relaxed state laws to retain their guns. In addition, many state domestic violence laws include the so-called boyfriend loophole, which often prevents authorities from confiscating firearms from an abusive dating partner who is not married to or cohabitating with the victim. March for Our Lives organizers called on Congress to protect women from gun violence by passing laws to disarm all domestic abusers.

Finally, March for Our Lives organizers sought legislation to prevent children from gaining access to guns left unsecured by adults. They pointed to the results of a 2015 national survey showing that 7 percent of American children, or 4.6 million individuals, live in homes where at least one firearm is kept loaded and unlocked. They argued that easy access to firearms in the home was associated with an increase in preventable deaths from accidental shootings and suicides. In addition, the student activists cited research showing that in 85 percent of school shootings—including the 2018 shooting that killed 10 people at Santa Fe High School in Texas—the perpetrators used guns belonging to their parents, other relatives, or friends (Cox and Rich 2018). The activists encouraged lawmakers to pass laws requiring safe and responsible firearm storage practices and imposing criminal liability on adults whose unsecured guns fall into the hands of children.

Further Reading

Axelrod, Tal. 2018. "California Shooter Used High-Capacity Magazine That Voters Outlawed, but Ban Was Blocked by Lawsuit." The Hill, November 9, 2018. https://thehill.com/homenews/news/415888-calif-shooter-used-high -capacity-magazine-that-ban-was.

Azrael, Deborah, Joanna Cohen, Carmel Salhi, and Matthew Miller. 2018. "Firearm Storage in Gun-Owning Households with Children: Results of a 2015 National Survey." *Journal of Urban Health* 95, no. 3 (2018): 295–304.

"The Background Check Loophole." 2018. Everytown for Gun Safety, April 21, 2018. https://everytownresearch.org/background-checks-loophole/.

Bryan, Bob. 2018. "Congress's Gigantic Spending Deal Looks Like It Will Change a 20-Year, NRA-Fueled Ban on Gun Violence Research." Business Insider, March 21, 2018. https://www.businessinsider.com/cdc-gun-violence-re search-ban-spending-bill-shutdown-2018-3.

Buchanan, Larry, Josh Keller, Richard A. Oppel Jr., and Daniel Victor. 2016. "How They Got Their Guns." *New York Times*, June 12, 2016. https:// www.nytimes.com/interactive/2015/10/03/us/how-mass-shooters-got -their-guns.html?_r=0.

Burrus, Trevor. 2018. "Let's Commit to Lowering Gun Deaths by 50 Percent in Ten Years. Will the Parkland Students' Proposals Help?" Cato Institute, March 27, 2018. https://www.cato.org/publications/commentary/lets-com mit-lowering-gun-deaths-50-percent-ten-years-will-parkland-students.

Chivers, C. J., Larry Buchanan, Denise Lu, and Karen Yourish. 2018. "With AR15s, Mass Shooters Attack with the Rifle Firepower Typically Used by Infantry Troops." *New York Times,* February 28, 2018. https://www

.nytimes.com/interactive/2018/02/28/us/ar-15-rifle-mass-shootings
.html.

Cox, John Woodrow, and Steven Rich. 2018. "Scarred by School Shootings." *Washington Post,* March 25, 2018. https://www.washingtonpost.com /graphics/2018/local/us-school-shootings-history/?utm_term=.311d4 c0661d5.

Freskos, Brian. 2018. "High-Capacity Magazines, Like the One Used by the California Mass Shooter, Are Deadly and Easily Available." The Trace, November 8, 2018. https://www.thetrace.org/2018/11/california-high-capacity -magazines-mass-shooting-handgun/.

Friedman, Dan. 2016. "The ATF's Nonsensical, Non-Traceable Gun Databases, Explained." The Trace, August 24, 2016. https://www.thetrace.org/2016 /08/atf-non-searchable-databases/.

Inskeep, Steve. 2015. "Ex-Rep. Dickey Regrets Restrictive Law on Gun Violence Research." National Public Radio, October 9, 2015. https://www.npr .org/2015/10/09/447098666/ex-rep-dickey-regrets-restrictive-law-on -gun-violence-research.

"Large Capacity Magazines." 2018. Giffords Law Center to Prevent Gun Violence. https://lawcenter.giffords.org/gun-laws/policy-areas/hardware-ammuni tion/large-capacity-magazines/.

Leahy, Patrick. 2018. "Leahy and Nelson Introduce the Crime Gun Tracing Modernization Act." Press release, U.S. Senate, May 24, 2018. https://www .leahy.senate.gov/press/leahy-and-nelson-introduce-the-crime-gun-trac ing-modernization-act.

Lopez, German. 2018. "The Capital Gazette Shooting and the Limits of an Assault Weapons Ban." Vox, June 29, 2018. https://www.vox.com/policy -and-politics/2018/4/3/17174160/assault-weapons-ar-15-ban.

MacBradaigh, Matt. 2013. "Gun Control Facts: Why a 'High Capacity' Magazine Ban Would Not Prevent Mass Shootings." Mic, January 30, 2013. https:// mic.com/articles/24263/gun-control-facts-why-a-high-capacity-maga zine-ban-would-not-prevent-mass-shootings#.Nhic2MLF2.

March for Our Lives. 2018. "Mission Statement." https://marchforourlives.com /mission-statement/.

Martinez, Michael. 2013. "'Universal Background Check': What Does It Mean?" CNN, January 28, 2013. https://www.cnn.com/2013/01/14/us/universal -background-checks/index.html.

McCarthy, Ciara. 2016. "Over 100 Medical Groups Urge Congress to Fund CDC Research on Gun Violence." *The Guardian,* April 6, 2016. https://www .theguardian.com/us-news/2016/apr/06/cdc-congress-research-gun-vio lence-public-health.

Mosher, Dave, and Skye Gould. 2018. "The Odds That a Gun Will Kill the Average American May Surprise You." Business Insider, October 29, 2018. https://www.businessinsider.com/us-gun-death-murder-risk-statistics -2018-3.

Pahn, Molly, Anita Knopov, and Michael Siegel. 2018. "Gun Violence in the U.S. Kills More Black People and Urban Dwellers." The Conversation, November 8, 2018. http://theconversation.com/gun-violence-in-the-us-kills-more -black-people-and-urban-dwellers-86825.

Shepard, Steven. 2018. "Gun Control Support Surges in Polls." Politico, February 28, 2018. https://www.politico.com/story/2018/02/28/gun-control-polling -parkland-430099.

Stark, David E., and Nigam H. Shah. 2017. "Funding and Publication of Research on Gun Violence and Other Leading Causes of Death." *Journal of the American Medical Association* 317, no. 1 (2017): 84–85. https://jamanet work.com/journals/jama/article-abstract/2595514.

"U.S. Support for Gun Control Tops 2–1, Highest Ever." 2018. Quinnipiac University Polling Institute, February 20, 2018. https://poll.qu.edu/national /release-detail?ReleaseID=2521.

Warner, Mark R. 2018. "I Voted against an Assault Weapons Ban. Here's Why I Changed My Mind." *Washington Post,* October 1, 2018. https://www .washingtonpost.com/opinions/i-voted-against-an-assault-weapons-ban -heres-why-i-changed-my-mind/2018/10/01/3bfa76a0-c594-11e8-9b1c -a90f1daae309_story.html?utm_term=.27f111f7b7c6.

Watkins, Ali. 2018. "How the NRA Keeps Federal Gun Regulators in Check." *New York Times,* February 22, 2018. https://www.nytimes.com/2018/02 /22/us/politics/trump-atf-nra.html.

Wing, Nick. 2018. "Banning High-Capacity Magazines Should Absolutely Be a Winnable Issue." Huffington Post, March 14, 2018. https://www.huffing tonpost.com/entry/high-capacity-magazine-ban_us_5aa843c9e4b0f7a6 89cd31ff.

School Safety and Proposals to Arm Teachers

March for Our Lives organizers argue that enacting comprehensive gun control legislation will help prevent mass shootings, ensuring that incidents such as the February 2018 shooting that took the lives of 17 of their classmates and teachers at Marjory Stoneman Douglas (MSD) High School in Parkland, Florida, will never happen again. Representatives of the National Rifle Association (NRA) and their allies in Congress contend that restricting access to firearms infringes on the Second Amendment rights of law-abiding gun owners without reducing gun violence. They suggest a number of other measures that they believe will improve school security and prevent school shootings, including a controversial proposal to arm the nation's teachers. Meanwhile, some critics assert that all the concern over school security is misplaced because school shootings are exceedingly rare. They claim that the extreme security measures already adopted in many schools—along with the media frenzy surrounding a few tragic incidents—have created a perception of danger that frightens parents and traumatizes children.

School Safety since Columbine

The intensive national focus on school safety and security arose in the wake of the 1999 mass shooting at Columbine High School in Littleton, Colorado. The Columbine massacre convinced countless schools across the United States to adopt new security measures aimed at preventing shootings, which has fundamentally changed the educational experiences of a generation of American students. As of 2015–2016, according to the National Center for Education Statistics, 94 percent of public schools restricted access to the building during school hours, up from 74 percent in 1999–2000. In addition to asking visitors to identify themselves or sign in, many schools installed security vestibules with bulletproof glass or required students to pass through metal detectors to enter the building. In addition, security cameras monitored more than 80 percent of school campuses in 2015–2016, compared to 19 percent before Columbine (National Center for Education Statistics 2017). Other commonly implemented security measures include requiring students to wear identification badges or carry their belongings in clear backpacks.

Since Columbine raised fears of school shootings, many districts have introduced regular school lockdowns and active-shooter drills to train students how to respond in emergency situations. Typical drills involve locking and barricading classroom doors, taping opaque material over windows, turning off lights, hiding in corners or closets, and taking cover underneath desks. Some schools train students to be aware of which classrooms have first-floor windows that can be used in case of an evacuation. Other schools have developed unusual, creative methods for using the element of surprise against intruders, such as encouraging students to keep canned goods in their desks and throw them in case of attack. "The canned food item could stun the intruder or even knock him out until the police arrive," administrators who adopted this approach at an Alabama middle school explained in a letter to parents. "The canned food item will give the students a sense of empowerment to protect themselves and will make them feel secure in case an intruder enters their classroom" (Toppo 2018).

Critics argue that the increases in security measures turn schools into virtual fortresses and create an unwarranted perception of danger in the minds of students and parents. Critics claim that active-shooter drills and related classroom preparations traumatize children and contribute to an atmosphere of fear that inhibits learning. "Schools are safe. They've been safe for a long time. They remain safe," said Northeastern University criminologist James Alan Fox. "If you surround kids with all sorts of security, it sends a message: 'There are bad guys out to get you'" (Toppo 2018). A *Washington Post* analysis confirmed that school shootings are extremely rare, occurring an average of 10 times per year over the 19 years between Columbine and MSD. Shootings that happened on school grounds and during school hours killed 143 students and staff members in that time period. Three of the deadliest mass shootings (at Columbine, MSD, and Sandy Hook Elementary School in Connecticut) inflated the death toll, accounting for 43 percent of the total (Cox and Rich 2018).

Research has shown that school-age Americans face far greater risks of death outside of school than at school. Of the nearly 32,500 reported deaths of children between 1999 and 2013, school shootings accounted for only 0.5 percent, while homicides, bicycle accidents, firearm accidents, falls, and drownings accounted for 98 percent (Toppo 2018). Despite their rarity, however, school shootings cause psychological damage to survivors who are exposed to gun violence. The *Washington Post* found that more than 187,000 students attended the 193 schools in 36 states and the District of Columbia that experienced shootings after Columbine, and that many of these young people developed long-lasting symptoms of anxiety and posttraumatic stress (Cox and Rich 2018). Pervasive media coverage of school shootings also exposes children to trauma and fuels their perception of constant danger. As a result, millions of young people across the United States live in fear of becoming the next victims of school shootings. "It's no longer the default that going to school is going to make you feel safe," said psychiatrist Bruce D. Perry. "Even kids who come from middle-class and upper-middle-class communities literally don't feel safe in schools" (Cox and Rich 2018).

Controversy over Arming Teachers

In the weeks following the MSD shooting, President Donald Trump and other Republican leaders largely ignored the March for Our Lives activists' demands for stricter gun control laws and instead focused their attention on measures intended to prevent school shootings by increasing building and campus security. On March 14—the day of the National School Walkout—the U.S. House of Representatives passed the Students, Teachers, and Officers Preventing (STOP) School Violence Act of 2018. The legislation set aside $50 million per year to help schools deter and respond to attacks by improving security infrastructure, implementing anonymous reporting systems for threats, and training students and staff members in crisis intervention. The Trump administration also expressed support for such measures as increasing access to mental health services for troubled youths and improving coordination between school administrators and law enforcement to identify and assess potential threats.

During a listening session with survivors of the MSD shooting, Trump promoted an NRA-backed proposal to "harden" the nation's schools by placing trained, armed defenders in buildings and classrooms—including security guards, resource officers, retired law enforcement personnel, military veterans, and teachers. He argued that maintaining gun-free zones around schools made them inviting targets for people with violent intentions, whereas the presence of armed teachers would serve as a deterrent. "This would only obviously be for people who are very adept at handling a gun. It's called concealed carry, where a teacher would have a concealed gun on them. They'd go for special training and they would be there and you would no longer have a gun-free zone," the president explained. "An attack has lasted, on average, about three minutes. It takes five to eight minutes for responders, for the police to come in, so the attack is over. If you had a teacher who was adept at firearms, they could very well end the attack very quickly" (Smith 2018). Administration officials noted that qualified teachers who volunteered to participate in the program would receive rigorous training from state and local law enforcement agencies.

The proposal to arm teachers came under immediate criticism from gun control advocates at the White House meeting. Nicole Hockley, who cofounded the gun violence prevention organization Sandy Hook Promise after her six-year-old son was killed in a 2012 shooting at his elementary school, told Trump that she opposed the idea. "Rather than arming them with a firearm, I would rather arm them with the knowledge of how to prevent these acts from happening in the first place," she stated. "Let's talk about prevention. There is so much that we can do to help people before it reaches that point, and I urge you please stay focused on that as well. It is the gun, it's the person behind the gun, and it's about helping people before they ever reach that point" (Smith 2018).

Trump's proposal also encountered resistance from the National Education Association, a union representing 3 million teachers in the United States. "Educators need to be focused on teaching our students," said the union's president, Lily Eskelsen Garcia. "We need solutions that will keep guns out of the hands of those who want to use them to massacre innocent children and educators. Arming teachers does nothing to prevent that" (Chuck and Siemaszko 2018). On social media, teachers across the country criticized the president's proposal to put guns in classrooms. Using the hashtag #ArmMeWith, they enumerated all the supplies they felt would be more valuable than guns in helping to educate their students.

Gun violence experts and school safety advocates also questioned whether arming teachers would deter school shooters or protect students. They noted that the NRA-backed proposal was based on the idea that "a good guy with a gun" could effectively intervene to stop "a bad guy with a gun." Although this idea is often articulated by gun rights groups, critics argue that it is poorly supported by evidence. They point out that some of the deadliest school shootings have happened on campuses that were patrolled by armed resource officers. At both Columbine and MSD, for instance, the shooters targeted the schools despite being aware of the presence of armed personnel (Sherman 2018). In the 193 school shootings examined by the *Washington Post,* an armed resource officer interceded to stop an active shooter in only 1 instance, outside of a California high school in 2001 (Cox and Rich 2018). Likewise, a Federal Bureau of Investigation review of 160 active-shooter situations between 2000 and 2013 revealed that the actions of an armed civilian only stopped 4 shootings, while the actions of unarmed civilians ended 21 incidents (Ho 2018).

The National Association of School Resource Officers (NASRO) also disagreed with the Trump administration's proposal to arm teachers. Leaders of the association noted that officers undergo extensive, ongoing training to avoid collateral damage while using firearms in high-stress situations and crowded environments. They worried that arming teachers would increase the risk of accidental shootings in schools, whether by teachers, by students who gained access to teachers' guns, or by law enforcement officers who mistook armed teachers for active shooters when responding to emergencies.

Public views about the idea of arming teachers tended to split along party lines. A Pew Research Center poll found that 69 percent of Republicans supported the proposal, compared to 26 percent of Democrats (Lopez 2018). Despite the controversy, the Florida legislature followed up on Trump's proposal by passing the Aaron Feis Guardian Act—named after a football coach who was killed in the MSD shooting—that earmarked $67 million in state funds to train interested teachers to carry guns in schools. The board of Broward County Public Schools, which includes MSD High School, quickly voted against participating in the program. "After an unspeakable tragedy, our district chose against further going down this potentially dangerous rabbit hole," said student survivor Ryan Deitsch (CBS News 2018).

Further Reading

CBS News. 2018. "Parkland School District Votes against Arming Teachers." CBS Interactive, April 10, 2018. https://www.cbsnews.com/news/parkland -school-shooting-arming-teachers-vote-today-2018-04-10/.

Chuck, Elizabeth, and Corky Siemaszko. 2018. "Trump's Proposal to Arm Teachers Panned by Experts as a 'Colossally Stupid Idea.'" NBC News, February 22, 2018. https://www.nbcnews.com/news/us-news/trump-s-propo sal-arm-teachers-panned-experts-colossally-stupid-idea-n850286.

Cox, John Woodrow, and Steven Rich. 2018. "Scarred by School Shootings." *Washington Post,* March 25, 2018. https://www.washingtonpost.com /graphics/2018/local/us-school-shootings-history/?utm_term=.311 d4c0661d5.

Ho, Shannon. 2018. "Despite NRA's Might, Students Hope This Is a 'Moment' for Gun Law Changes." NBC 7 San Diego, March 23, 2018. https://www .nbcsandiego.com/news/politics/March-for-Our-Lives-Gun-Policy -Change-NRA-477221293.html.

Lopez, German. 2018. "Why the March for Our Lives Could Win." Vox, March 26, 2018. https://www.vox.com/policy-and-politics/2018/3/24/17158592 /march-for-our-lives-gun-control-nra.

National Center for Education Statistics. 2017. "Table 233.50: Percentage of Public Schools with Various Safety and Security Measures." Digest of Education Statistics. https://nces.ed.gov/programs/digest/d17/tables/dt17_233 .50.asp.

Sherman, Amy. 2018. "How Do We Prevent School Shootings?" PolitiFact, February 15, 2018. https://www.politifact.com/truth-o-meter/article/2018 /feb/15/how-do-we-prevent-school-shootings/.

Smith, David. 2018. "Trump's Solution to School Shootings: Arm Teachers with Guns." *The Guardian,* February 21, 2018. https://www.theguardian.com /us-news/2018/feb/21/donald-trump-solution-to-school-shootings-arm -teachers-with-guns.

Toppo, Greg. 2018. "20 Years In, Shootings Have Changed Schools in Unexpected Ways." *USA Today,* January 24, 2018. https://www.usatoday.com /story/news/2018/01/24/20-years-school-shootings-loom-large-public -imagination/1063337001/.

A New Age of Youth Activism

The March for Our Lives attracted an estimated 2 million participants, making it one of the largest youth-led protests in U.S. history. Student survivors of the February 2018 shooting at Marjory Stoneman Douglas (MSD) High School in Parkland, Florida, galvanized members of their generation to demand legislative action to prevent gun violence. Some observers placed the student organizers within a tradition of youth activism that began during the social unrest of the 1960s, which included antiwar protests on college campuses during the Vietnam War (1955–1975) and marches and sit-ins against racial segregation during the civil rights movement. Others viewed the Never Again movement as part of a new age of youth activism for the twenty-first century, along with such social media–driven campaigns as #BlackLivesMatter and #MeToo. "We're in a groundswell moment of youth activism," said Meira Levinson, a professor of civic and multicultural education at Harvard University (Jason 2018).

The March for Our Lives mobilized young Americans who felt frustrated by two decades of political inaction toward solving the problem of school shootings. Parkland survivors described themselves as part of the "mass shooting generation"—children raised and educated in a world shaped by the 1999 Columbine High School massacre, with school lockdowns, active-shooter drills, security cameras, and armed school resource officers as their daily reality. A *Washington Post* study determined that more than 187,000 U.S. students had experienced a shooting at school since Columbine (Cox and Rich 2018), creating a responsive audience for the Parkland students' message. "I have followed school shootings since Columbine, nearly 19 years ago, and I've never seen anything like the #NeverAgain kids," wrote Dave Cullen, author of a book analyzing the Columbine shooting. "It's radically different this time. . . . It's about the right people with the right standing, in the right moment, just picking up the ball and running with it. . . . The Parkland kids were hunted, ran for their lives, again, and then called BS, literally, on the big deadly lie that we can't allow hunting and still protect our kids" (Cullen 2018).

In addition to applying pressure on Congress for comprehensive gun control legislation, the Never Again student activists led a nationwide drive aimed at convincing their peers to register and vote. They planned to use their collective power to influence election outcomes, unseat politicians who accepted campaign contributions from the National Rifle Association (NRA), and elect candidates who supported commonsense gun regulation. The March for Our Lives marked the first step in mobilizing their generation to chart a future without school shootings. "Our history is defined by the youthful push to make America more just, more compassionate, more equal under the law. This generation—of Parkland, of Dreamers, of Black Lives Matter—embraces that duty," former president Barack Obama declared. "If they make their elders uncomfortable, that's how it should be. Our kids now show us what we've told them America is all about, even if we haven't always believed it ourselves: that our future isn't written for us, but by us" (Obama 2018).

Building on Historic Precedent

Young activists led some of the most potent social change movements of the twentieth century. Student activism played a vital role in the civil rights movement beginning in 1960, when 4 African American college freshmen staged a sit-in protest at a segregated Woolworth's lunch counter in Greensboro, North Carolina, sparking a nationwide boycott. In 1963, around 1,000 children and teenagers skipped school to join a march against segregation in Birmingham, Alabama. News footage of young people being sprayed by fire hoses and threatened by snarling police dogs generated public outrage and forced the city to desegregate. In 1964, members of the Student Nonviolent Coordinating Committee led a campaign to register black voters in the South as a means of promoting change. The Parkland students took many cues from the civil rights movement, adopting its nonviolent protest tactics as well as its focus on voter registration. They highlighted the connection by featuring a speech by Yolanda Renee King, the nine-year-old granddaughter of civil rights leader Martin Luther King Jr., at the March for Our Lives.

Some observers compared the Never Again movement to the antiwar protests that rocked college campuses during the Vietnam War era. Like the antiwar movement held personal significance for people of draft age, the March for Our Lives resonated with a generation of students raised with the expectation of gun violence. "One of the reasons why the protest movement against the Vietnam War in the 1960s was so massive is that everyone was exposed to this universal draft and there was a real danger to [men] that might be drafted," Columbia University professor Ed Morales explained. "Now, we're at this place where mass shootings are so common that young people feel [shootings] are almost as much a threat to their lives" (Mejia 2018).

The March for Our Lives also built upon a surge in social concern, political awareness, and organized protest in the twenty-first century, including the Black Lives Matter movement for racial justice and the #MeToo movement against sexual assault. A 2016 survey of undergraduate students found that 10 percent planned to participate in political demonstrations during their college years, which represented the largest percentage since 1967 (Jason 2018). Some observers claimed that the Parkland students' socioeconomic background—coming from an affluent, highly educated, mostly white suburban community—brought a higher level of media attention and political responsiveness to their cause. Florida governor Rick Scott agreed to meet with the activists within a week of the MSD shooting, for instance, and signed a new gun safety bill into law on March

9, 2018. In contrast, Scott refused to meet with the Dream Defenders—a group of African American activists seeking to overturn Florida's controversial stand-your-ground law that led to an acquittal in the shooting death of unarmed black teenager Trayvon Martin—even after they staged a monthlong protest at the state capitol in 2013.

Another element that distinguished the Never Again movement from its predecessors was the student activists' effective use of modern social media tools to reach a mass audience. As the MSD shooter stalked the halls of the school, student journalist David Hogg pulled out his cell phone and interviewed his classmates while they hid in a locked storeroom. Dozens of other Parkland students took photographs to document their experiences during the shooting and posted them on Snapchat. MSD junior Cameron Kasky expressed his anger on social media in the hours after the shooting and encouraged fellow survivors to use the hashtag #NeverAgain. After her speech at a February 17 gun control rally went viral, senior Emma González opened a Twitter account and quickly surpassed 1 million followers. The Never Again activists employed both social media and the mainstream news media as organizing tools to spread their message, advocate for change, mobilize young supporters, encourage political engagement, and shape the national conversation about gun control. They also organized consumer boycotts that convinced a slew of large corporations to sever their relationships with the NRA.

Voting for Change

The Never Again activists recognized that electing leaders who supported their interests provided the key to turning their activism into meaningful legislative action and reducing NRA influence on the political system. After the school year ended in the spring of 2018, a group of Parkland students embarked on nationwide bus tour aimed at registering young voters and encouraging them to participate in the fall midterm elections. The Road to Change tour also featured a diverse group of student activists from urban communities that were disproportionately affected by gun violence. "We're going to make this the voting issue. We're going to take this to every election, to every state and every city," Hogg stated. "To those politicians supported by the NRA that allow the continued slaughter of our children and our future, I say get your résumés ready" (Hogg 2018). By the time the tour concluded in August, 77 percent of voters between the ages of 18 and 29 indicated that candidates' positions on gun control would play an important role in their decisions (Miller 2018).

The results of the November midterm elections suggested that concern about school shootings contributed to a political awakening among young voters. Exit polls showed that 31 percent of Americans between the ages of 18 and 29 cast ballots, up from 21 percent in 2014 and the highest level in nearly three decades. Young voters favored Democratic candidates, who tend to support gun control measures, over Republicans by a 35-point margin (Hansen 2018). In focus groups of young voters leading up to the midterm elections, Harvard University professor John Della Volpe reported that school shootings topped a list of 16 issues cited by participants as contributing to an increase in civic engagement. "Gun violence was in the top five, but school shooting in particular is what stood out for a majority of young Americans," he stated (Booker 2018).

Opinions varied on the degree to which greater participation by young voters affected the outcome of the elections. The NRA Political Victory Fund pointed to the Parkland activists' home state of Florida, where gun rights candidates prevailed in elections for governor and U.S. Senate, as evidence that the March for Our Lives did not change voters' minds. "Florida voters rejected the extreme gun control agenda," chairman Chris Cox asserted, "and sent a clear message in support of our Second Amendment right to self-defense" (Keierleber 2018). The Never Again activists refused to be discouraged and vowed to continue fighting for gun reform. "Things didn't necessarily go our way, but we know that this is the start, that it's going to be a long road," Hogg acknowledged. "The Florida elections were very close, which is encouraging. For us, the loss in Florida is a call to action" (Keierleber 2018).

Nationally, the student-led movement against gun violence also achieved mixed results. Analysts noted that 74 percent of the 144 congressional candidates who received the most NRA campaign funding won election to office. At the same time, though, they found that 68 percent of the 129 congressional candidates backed by the gun control group Giffords won their elections (Keierleber 2018). Nevertheless, the outcomes of a few high-profile races convinced many observers that the March for Our Lives had resulted in a significant shift in the national debate over gun regulation. They cited victories by Democratic candidates who expressed support for commonsense gun reform over Republican candidates with long-standing "A" ratings from the NRA in such states as Texas, Kansas, and Georgia, where advocating gun control would have doomed a candidate's political aspirations in the past. In addition, supporters of the Never Again movement predicted that young voters would have an even greater impact on the 2020 presidential election, when the 90 million millennials of voting age will make up nearly 40 percent of the U.S. electorate (Hansen 2018).

Since many youth movements from earlier eras have proven to be short-lived—faltering when charismatic and influential student leaders graduated and moved on to other endeavors—some critics questioned whether the March for Our Lives organizers could sustain their momentum through 2020 and beyond. "Because the status quo is always going to have more money and political power, failure is an inevitable, and in some ways essential, part of youth movements," said Marshall Ganz of Harvard's Kennedy School of Government. "The challenge is to turn them into learning opportunities and have the moral resources for the resilience that it takes to do that." Nevertheless, he noted, "Young people come of age with three tools essential for renewal: a critical eye of the world, a clear view of its needs and pain, and hopeful hearts that give a sense of the world's promise and possibilities" (Jason 2018).

Further Reading

Booker, Brakkton. 2018. "After Parkland, Young Voters Were Galvanized, Activists Vow to Continue to Organize." National Public Radio, November 8, 2018. https://www.npr.org/2018/11/08/665547189/youth-vote-and-gun -control-in-florida.

Cox, John Woodrow, and Steven Rich. 2018. "Scarred by School Shootings." *Washington Post,* March 25, 2018. https://www.washingtonpost.com /graphics/2018/local/us-school-shootings-history/?utm_term=.311d4 c0661d5.

Cullen, Dave. 2018. "'The News Forgets. Very Quickly.' Inside the Marjory Stoneman Douglas Students' Incredible Race to Make History." *Vanity Fair,* March 7, 2018. https://www.vanityfair.com/news/2018/03/inside-the -marjory-stoneman-douglas-students-race-to-make-history.

Hansen, Claire. 2018. "Young Voters Turned Out in Historic Numbers, Early Estimates Show." *U.S. News and World Report,* November 7, 2018. https:// www.usnews.com/news/politics/articles/2018-11-07/young-voters -turned-out-in-historic-numbers-early-estimates-show.

Hogg, David. 2018. "March for Our Lives: Stoneman Douglas Student David Hogg's Speech." NBC News, March 24, 2018. https://www.nbcnews.com /video/march-for-our-lives-stoneman-douglas-student-david-hogg-s -speech-1194238019932?v=railb&.

Jason, Zachary. 2018. "Student Activism 2.0." *Harvard Ed.,* Fall. https://www.gse .harvard.edu/news/ed/18/08/student-activism-20.

Keierleber, Mark. 2018. "Despite Post-Parkland Surge in Youth Vote, Student Activists Largely Fail to Oust Pro-Gun Candidates in Midterms." The 74, November 8, 2018. https://www.the74million.org/despite-post-parkland -surge-in-youth-vote-student-activists-largely-fail-to-oust-pro-gun-can didates-in-midterms/.

Mejia, Zameena. 2018. "How the March for Our Lives Gen Z Organizers Changed the Gun Control Conversation When No One Else Could." CNBC Make It, March 24, 2018. https://www.cnbc.com/2018/03/23/how-the-march -for-our-lives-organizers-changed-the-gun-control-conversation.html.

Miller, Lisa. 2018. "David Hogg, after Parkland." New York Magazine, August 19, 2018. http://nymag.com/intelligencer/2018/08/david-hogg-is-taking-his -gap-year-at-the-barricades.html.

Obama, Barack. 2018. "Cameron Kasky, Jaclyn Corin, David Hogg, Emma González, and Alex Wind." *Time*, April 19, 2018. http://time.com/collec tion/most-influential-people-2018/5217568/parkland-students/.

Salamon, Errol. 2018. "March for Our Lives Awakens the Spirit of Student and Media Activism from the 1960s." The Conversation, March 23, 2018. https://theconversation.com/march-for-our-lives-awakens-the-spirit-of -student-and-media-activism-of-the-1960s-93713.

A Shift in Public Sentiments about Gun Control

The incident at Marjory Stoneman Douglas (MSD) High School in Parkland, Florida, on February 14, 2018, was neither the first nor the worst U.S. school shooting. By the time a gunman killed 17 students and staff members at the school, mass shootings seemed to occur with such regularity that one incident had barely receded from the headlines before the next one occurred. Within the four months prior to Parkland, for instance, a gunman murdered 58 people at an outdoor music festival in Las Vegas, Nevada, and another shooter killed 26 people at a Baptist church near San Antonio, Texas. The string of shootings left many Americans with a sense of resignation that no amount of gun violence could break through the long-standing political stalemate between supporters of gun control and gun rights. The MSD shooting initially appeared unlikely to alter this pattern.

Within hours of the Parkland shooting, however, student survivors began speaking out and demanding change in a forceful, coordinated manner. Unlike the gun control activism that had followed previous school shootings, the student-led Never Again movement seemed to impact public sentiment and shift the national debate. The MSD survivors raised awareness, inflamed passions, and turned gun violence prevention into a defining issue for a generation of young people. The broad reach of the Parkland organizers' message became apparent at the March for Our Lives, which mobilized an estimated 2 million participants in Washington, D.C., and 800 satellite marches elsewhere in the United States and around the world. "A tipping point was finally reached in the drive for gun sanity," declared a writer for the *New Yorker*. "The eloquence of the testimony by the survivors of the Parkland massacre and the authority of their witness might, one imagines, finally turn the ever more despairing national debate about gun control around" (Gopnik 2018).

Increasing Support for Gun Control

The March for Our Lives generated a significant increase in public support for gun control. A Politico/Morning Consult survey of registered voters found that 68 percent favored stricter gun control laws, while only 25 percent opposed tighter restrictions on firearms. This marked the highest level of support for gun control in 25 years—since Congress passed the Brady Handgun Violence Prevention Act and the federal assault weapons ban in 1994. Researchers noted that Republican voters accounted for much of the increase, with the percentage of Republicans expressing support for gun control surging from 37 percent in 2016 to 53 percent following the Parkland shooting (Gray 2018).

Polls also showed widespread bipartisan agreement on several of the specific gun control measures promoted by March for Our Lives organizers. "Congress's inaction on guns over the past few years is not due to the unpopularity of gun control measures," wrote Vox analyst German Lopez. "If you look at the polling, support for gun control, depending on which specific measure respondents are asked about, can be *very* high among both Democrats and Republicans. . . . There's a lot of remarkable middle ground" (Lopez 2018). A Pew Research Center survey found equivalent levels of support, at 89 percent, among Democrats and Republicans for policies intended to prevent people with mental health issues from obtaining firearms. Voters of both parties also overwhelmingly approved of requiring universal background checks for all gun sales, with 90 percent of Democrats and 77 percent Republicans favoring such measures. A majority from both parties also expressed support for banning the sale of assault weapons and creating a digitized federal database to track firearm transactions (Lopez 2018).

Despite their popularity with voters, such measures failed to gain traction in Congress over the years because few people felt strongly enough about gun control to make it their primary voting issue. Gun rights advocates, on the other hand, were more politically active, expressing vocal opposition to gun control by contacting public officials, contributing to the National Rifle Association (NRA), and voting for candidates who support the Second Amendment. The Never Again movement sought to change this dynamic by registering young voters and voting NRA-backed politicians out of office. The activists boosted the level of issue intensity around gun violence prevention and exerted pressure on lawmakers to meet their demands. "For once, we are seeing a mass movement that is *extremely* dedicated to gun control," Lopez noted. "And by attracting so much national attention, the movement may inspire other Americans to follow suit, making gun control an issue that can actually sway votes" (Lopez 2018).

The growing political power of the Never Again movement became clear in the 2018 midterm elections. For many years, the NRA had indicated its level of support for political candidates on its website by giving them letter grades ranging from "A" to "F." In previous elections, many candidates across the country touted their lifetime "A" ratings from the gun lobby in their campaigns. Prior to the 2018 midterms, however, the NRA removed the letter grades from its website. The gun violence prevention group Everytown for Gun Safety reposted the information online, describing the NRA endorsement as a "scarlet letter" that should make voters reconsider backing those candidates. In a reversal of the former situation, some Democratic candidates made their lifetime "F" ratings prominent features of their campaigns.

Everytown and Giffords, a gun control organization founded by former congresswoman and mass shooting victim Gabby Giffords, spent $37 million to influence voters during the 2018 midterms, nearly doubling the $20 million spent by the NRA (Hakim and Shorey 2018). As a result, gun control advocacy made up 59 percent of campaign advertising, compared to 31 percent in 2016 and 11 percent in 2014 (Bonazzo 2018). Although the election results were mixed, with both sides expressing pleasure or disappointment in the outcomes of various races, gun control emerged as an important issue for many voters. Democratic challengers backed by Giffords defeated four incumbent Republican U.S. House members with NRA "A" ratings in Texas, Colorado, Virginia, and Minnesota, while Democrats backed by Everytown won 15 of 16 races against Republican incumbents. "The NRA remains a potent force in American politics," noted a *New York Times* analysis. "But the NRA has also arguably gained its most formidable counterweight since its emergence as a modern political force in the late 1970s" (Hakim and Shorey 2018).

Declining Influence of the NRA

The Parkland activists made the NRA and its powerful influence over American politics a major focus of the March for Our Lives. They argued that a small but vocal group of gun rights extremists had hijacked the national conversation about gun control and blocked the passage of commonsense measures to reduce gun violence in the United States. They blamed the gun lobby, along with elected officials who accepted campaign contributions from the NRA, for the lack of government action to protect children from school shootings. The Never Again activists "called BS" on NRA assertions that expanding access to guns made people safer and that limiting gun rights threatened American values. "People are trying to spin what we're doing, saying we're out to take away their Second Amendment rights," said Parkland student survivor Chris Grady. "Our main goal is to save kids' lives, people's lives. This is a public safety issue that takes place in concerts, churches, airports, not just schools" (Ho 2018). When NRA leaders pushed back, the student activists organized boycotts that convinced several large companies to sever their relationship with the NRA.

The March for Our Lives helped shift public opinion against the NRA. A survey of 1,100 active voters from both political parties conducted in the fall of 2018 found that a majority held an unfavorable view of the NRA as "a political organization that fights to weaken gun laws." Although the NRA's popularity typically declines in the aftermath of mass shootings, the polls suggested that its support failed to rebound after the Parkland shooting. "It's changed from a popular organization that politicians feared to an unpopular organization that politicians try to distance themselves from," said pollster Margie Omero. "For a lot of Americans, it's reached a tipping point. This group is standing in the way of popular action" (Bonazzo 2018).

With between 5 million and 6 million members, the NRA represents about 20 percent of the nation's gun owners. Yet NRA members are among the most passionate and motivated defenders of gun rights. NRA leaders presented the March for Our Lives as a serious threat to gun rights and used it to mobilize members. "Wake up people and see what's happening!" NRA board member Charles Cotton posted online. "[Everytown for Gun Safety founder Michael] Bloomberg and Hollywood are pouring money into this effort and the media is helping to the fullest extent. We've never had this level of opposition before, not ever. It's a campaign of lies and distortion, but it's very well funded and they are playing on the sympathy factor of kids getting killed. If you really want to make a difference, then start recruiting NRA members every single day" (Abramson 2018).

The NRA's Political Victory Fund collected $2.4 million in contributions in March 2018, which represented its highest monthly total in 18 years. "The NRA sends out messaging to say we are under attack. Your rights are under attack. The antigun people are coming to take away your guns," political scientist Robert J. Spitzer explained. "The fear-based appeal is the most successful way to raise money. When political events go against them, they tend to do better" (Swisher and Chokey 2018). Despite the influx of donations, the NRA's financial situation did not appear secure. In legal briefs filed with a New York court in the fall of 2018, NRA attorneys claimed that the organization faced a financial crisis that threatened its continued existence. "If the NRA is unable to collect donations from its members, safeguard the assets endowed to it, apply its funds to cover media buys and other expenses integral to its political speech, and obtain basic corporate insurance coverage, it will be unable to exist as a not-for-profit or pursue its advocacy mission" (Hayes 2018). Parkland activists responded to news of the NRA's struggles by sarcastically offering "thoughts and prayers" on social media.

The March for Our Lives message resonated with many Americans who felt increasingly frustrated with political inaction on gun violence. Nevertheless, polls showed that many voters continued to feel pessimistic about the chances that Congress would pass meaningful gun control legislation. Only 10 percent of respondents in the Politico/Morning Consult survey described the chances as "excellent," while 32 percent said the chances were "poor" (Gray 2018). Never Again activists pledged to continue mobilizing their peers and registering young voters in order to elect future leaders who would be more responsive to their demands. "The best consequence of the students' movement isn't likely to be the effect that it has on legislatures as they now exist," said a *New Yorker* writer. "It will be on the next legislatures, as they exist after the next elections, and those that follow after that" (Gopnik 2018).

Further Reading

Abramson, Alana. 2018. "Membership in Gun Groups Is Spiking after the Florida Shooting." *Time,* March 2, 2018. http://time.com/5176471/national-rifle-association-membership-florida-shooting/.

Bonazzo, John. 2018. "NRA Slipping with Voters, though Many Have Moved On from Gun Control." Observer, September 10, 2018. https://observer.com/2018/09/nra-gun-control-polling-parkland/.

Gopnik, Adam. 2018. "Two Views on the March for Our Lives and the Second Amendment." *New Yorker,* March 29, 2018. https://www.newyorker.com/news/daily-comment/two-views-on-the-march-for-our-lives-and-the-second-amendment.

Gray, Sarah. 2018. "Gun Control Support Has Surged to Its Highest Level in 25 Years." *Time,* February 28, 2018. http://time.com/5180006/gun-control-support-has-surged-to-its-highest-level-in-25-years/.

Hakim, Danny, and Rachel Shorey. 2018. "Gun Control Groups Eclipse NRA in Election Spending." *New York Times,* November 16, 2018. https://www.nytimes.com/2018/11/16/us/politics/nra-gun-control-fund-raising.html.

Hayes, Christal. 2018. "NRA Says It Faces Financial Crisis, Claims It Might Be 'Unable to Exist' in Future." *USA Today,* August 3, 2018. https://www.usatoday.com/story/news/politics/2018/08/03/nra-faces-financial-crisis-claims-might-unable-exist/902918002/.

Ho, Shannon. 2018. "Despite NRA's Might, Students Hope This Is a 'Moment' for Gun Law Changes." NBC 7 San Diego, March 23, 2018. https://www.nbcsandiego.com/news/politics/March-for-Our-Lives-Gun-Policy-Change-NRA-477221293.html.

Lopez, German. 2018. "Why the March for Our Lives Could Win." Vox, March 26, 2018. https://www.vox.com/policy-and-politics/2018/3/24/17158592/march-for-our-lives-gun-control-nra.

Swisher, Skyler, and Aric Chokey. 2018. "The NRA Broke a Fundraising Record after Parkland. Will That Sway Elections?" *Sun-Sentinel,* April 27, 2018. https://www.sun-sentinel.com/local/palm-beach/fl-reg-nra-record-month-20180426-story.html.

CHAPTER FOUR

Profiles

This chapter provides illuminating biographical profiles of important figures in the Never Again movement and the larger gun control debate, including March for Our Lives student organizers Emma González and David Hogg; gun control advocates Michael Bloomberg, Gabby Giffords, and Shannon Watts; and gun rights defenders Wayne LaPierre and Dana Loesch.

Mark Barden (1965?–)

Gun violence prevention advocate and cofounder of Sandy Hook Promise

A native of New York, Mark Barden worked as a session guitarist in Nashville, Tennessee, for many years. He also toured nationally with country, bluegrass, and popular music artists, including Michael Martin Murphey, Doug Stone, and the Cox Family. Barden married Jacqueline Giblin, a second-grade teacher, and they had three children, James, Natalie, and Daniel. After house-sitting for family members nearby, Barden and his wife decided to move to Newtown, Connecticut, around 2008. They were attracted by its friendly, small-town environment as well as its excellent public school system.

During the 2012 school year, the Barden children attended three different schools. After playing musical gigs until late at night, Barden still got up early in the morning to spend time with each child before their school bus arrived. The youngest, seven-year-old Daniel, attended Sandy Hook Elementary School, where he was known as a happy, caring, considerate boy. "His teachers would always comment on how he was always looking after his classmates," Barden recalled. "He would go talk to somebody that was sitting alone. If he saw somebody struggling with something, he'd offer his help. We just heard that consistently all the way through" (Childress 2013).

On December 14, 2012, a gunman armed with an AR-15 semiautomatic rifle forced his way into Sandy Hook Elementary School and murdered 20 first-grade students and 6 educators. Barden rushed to the school, where he waited several hours for news of Daniel. "When I arrived on the scene, it was overwhelming, the number of emergency vehicles and military personnel and helicopters," he remembered. "At our little Sandy Hook School, which is quaint, bucolic, down-a-country-road little school where I knew everybody because I was in there volunteering fairly regularly, and it was just such a comfortable little quiet environment, and to see it transformed into a chaotic emergency scene was surreal" (Childress 2013).

After most of the anxious parents were reunited with their children, Barden learned that Daniel did not survive the shooting. "This sweet little boy, the caretaker of all living things, the light of happiness in our little family was among those 20 first-grade children who had been shot to death," he said. "During those first weeks, my wife Jackie and I would be collapsed literally on the floor in a heap, just sobbing and crying . . . whispering to each other, 'I just want to die'" (Brooks 2017b). With the support of many people in the Newtown community, though, Barden eventually decided to honor Daniel's memory by turning his profound grief into political action. "I have an opportunity to effect change and prevent this from happening to another family," Barden noted. "I can't *not* do that. I don't have a choice" (Brooks 2017a).

Along with other Newtown parents, Barden cofounded the nonprofit organization Sandy Hook Promise (SHP). He served as its managing director and one of its main spokespeople. Immediately after its founding, SHP joined other gun control advocacy organizations in calling for legislation to expand federal background checks to cover firearm purchases made online and at gun shows. The bipartisan Public Safety and Second Amendment Rights Protection Act, known informally as the Manchin-Toomey Amendment, was defeated in the Senate after the National Rifle Association (NRA) and other gun rights groups spent millions of dollars opposing it. "I didn't think it was going to be so contentious and difficult," Barden acknowledged. "I just figured, well of course that's something everyone can get behind—that everyone should have a background check before they purchase a firearm. And the reality is that about 90 percent of Americans agree. . . . It's inside the halls of Congress where that common sense and logic seem to break down" (Bologna 2017).

Following that defeat, SHP shifted its focus toward teaching people about the causes of gun violence and providing them with tools to help prevent it. SHP trained millions of students, educators, and parents to recognize the warning signs of individuals who may be at risk for gun violence and to intervene before they hurt themselves or other people. Barden noted that the perpetrator of the Sandy Hook shooting exhibited many warning signs prior to the massacre, which might have been prevented if he had received help. "One of the things I lay awake at night still thinking about is that the guy that shot and killed my sweet little Daniel was horribly, chronically socially isolated," he stated. "If somebody like Daniel had maybe one more conversation with that guy he could've made the whole difference" (Stein 2017).

In January 2016, Barden testified before the Senate in hearings about how to prevent gun violence. "I am before you today as a grieving father who knows firsthand the cost of inaction," he declared. "I'm asking you to think of my sweet little Daniel and what was lost here . . . and the 90 American families who will lose a loved one today, and another 90 tomorrow . . . and so on every day until we do something" (Barden 2016). Barden also met with President Barack Obama, and later President Donald Trump, to discuss possible solutions to school shootings. In 2018 Barden considered running for the U.S. House of Representatives from Connecticut's Fifth District, representing the northwestern part of the state, after Democratic representative Elizabeth Esty retired in the midst of allegations that she mishandled a harassment issue involving her staff.

When a gunman killed 17 people at Marjory Stoneman Douglas High School in Parkland, Florida, in February 2018, Barden expressed support and admiration for the surviving students who launched the Never Again movement on social media and organized the March for Our Lives. The outspoken student activists confronted politicians who accepted donations from the NRA and convinced several large corporations to stop offering discounts to NRA members. "What a force to be reckoned with," Barden said of the Parkland students. "They are protecting their own future. They are not going to be intimidated by corporate greed. They're not going to be bullied by money and power" (Gstalter 2018).

Further Reading

Barden, Mark. 2016. "Statement of Mr. Mark Barden, Founder and Managing Director of Sandy Hook Promise, before the U.S. Senate." Sandy Hook Promise, January 20, 2016. https://www.sandyhookpromise.org/state ment_of_mark_barden_before_the_united_states_senate.

Bologna, Caroline. 2017. "Six Parents of Sandy Hook Shooting Victims on Moving Forward after Unspeakable Loss." Huffington Post, December 14, 2017. https://www.huffingtonpost.com/entry/sandy-hook-victims-5-years_us _5a2ac6cce4b073789f695659.

Brooks, Anthony. 2017a. "Five Years after Sandy Hook School Shooting, a Father Honors His Son." WBUR News, December 6, 2017. http://www.wbur.org /radioboston/2017/12/06/sandy-hook-father.

Brooks, Anthony. 2017b. "Two Fathers Who Lost Their Sons in School Shootings Transform Their Grief into Action." WBUR News, October 17, 2017. http://www.wbur.org/news/2017/10/17/guns-grief-barden-gibson.

Childress, Sarah. 2013. "Jackie and Mark Barden, Parents of Newtown Victim: 'Daniel Was a Kind Little Soul.'" PBS, February 19, 2013. https://www .pbs.org/wgbh/frontline/article/jackie-and-mark-barden-parents-of -newtown-victim-daniel-was-a-kind-little-soul/.

Gstalter, Morgan. 2018. "Newtown Father Praises Parkland Students as 'A Force to be Reckoned With.'" The Hill, February 23, 2018. http://thehill.com /blogs/blog-briefing-room/news/375341-newtown-father-praises-park land-students-as-a-force-to-be.

Stein, Joshua David. 2017. "Mark Barden's Son Won't Be the Last Child Gunned Down." Fatherly, October 9, 2017. https://www.fatherly.com/love-money /culture/mark-barden-sandy-hook-promise-gun-violence/.

Michael Bloomberg (1942–)

Former mayor of New York City and cofounder of Everytown for Gun Safety

Born in Boston, Massachusetts, on February 14, 1942, to William Henry Bloomberg and Charlotte Bloomberg, Michael Bloomberg spent his formative years in Medford, Massachusetts. In 1958 he became one of the youngest boys in the country to achieve the rank of Eagle Scout from the Boy Scouts of America. Bloomberg paid his own way through college at Johns Hopkins University by working as a parking attendant and taking out student loans. After earning a bachelor's degree from Johns Hopkins in 1964, he enrolled at the Harvard Business School and received a master's degree in business administration in 1966.

That same year, Bloomberg accepted an entry-level position at Salomon Brothers, a Wall Street investment firm. He quickly rose through the ranks to become head of the company's information systems. In 1981, Salomon Brothers merged with the Phibro Corporation. Bloomberg left the company after 15 years of employment and received a significant severance package. He used that money to start his own business buying and selling financial securities. From its beginnings in a one-room office, that company eventually became Bloomberg LP, a financial media empire that employed more than 19,000 people in over 176 locations around the world. Bloomberg became a billionaire and one of the most prominent businessmen in New York City.

In 2002, Bloomberg was elected mayor of New York City. After winning reelection to a second term in 2005, he left the Republican Party and registered as an Independent. Voters elected him to a third term in office in 2008. During his tenure, Bloomberg received credit for improving New York City's public school system, spurring economic growth, increasing tourism, and reducing unemployment. Even after a crash in the housing market sparked a recession in 2008, the city experienced record-level job growth in the private sector. Bloomberg also garnered national recognition for launching such antipoverty measures as the Young Men's Initiative and the Center for Economic Opportunity. The federal government's Social Innovation Fund created an $85 million competitive grant program to replicate the success of Bloomberg's initiatives in other cities. Bloomberg also implemented an indoor smoking ban in public places that was soon adopted across the country.

After serving three terms in office, Bloomberg returned to the private sector and devoted much of his time and wealth to philanthropic endeavors. Bloomberg Philanthropies, which he founded in 2004, funds initiatives designed to create lasting change in five areas: public health, environment, education, government innovation, and arts and culture. In 2006, Bloomberg partnered with former Boston mayor Thomas Menino to form Mayors Against Illegal Guns, a group comprising more than 1,000 mayors from nearly every state who advocated reform of the nation's gun laws.

In 2012, a gunman entered Sandy Hook Elementary School in Newtown, Connecticut—about 60 miles from New York City—and killed 26 people, including 20 first-grade students ages six and seven years old. Bloomberg responded to the tragedy by publishing an opinion piece titled "Six Ways to Stop Gun Madness: Steps Obama Should Take to Make Real Changes. Our Kids Deserve It." The article proposed a series of legislative changes, such as strengthening background checks and banning the sale of military-style assault weapons, that he claimed were necessary to prevent mass shootings. "For more than a decade, both parties in Washington have mostly looked the other way when mass shootings occur. And they have mostly ignored the 34 victims who are murdered with guns every single day," Bloomberg declared. "And there is no escaping the fact that we must do more to protect our communities from gun violence" (Bloomberg 2012).

In 2014, Mayors Against Illegal Guns partnered with Moms Demand Action for Gun Sense in America to form the nonprofit organization Everytown for Gun Safety. Largely funded by Bloomberg, the organization criticized the gun lobby for its opposition to what Everytown referred to as commonsense gun laws, such as universal background checks for gun purchases. In 2014, Bloomberg offered to match every donation given to the organization to combat gun violence. "I think there's no leadership on keeping guns out of the hands of criminals, minors, and people with psychiatric problems, which this country should be ashamed that we're not doing," he stated (Brennan 2018).

In 2015, after nine people were gunned down at Umpqua Community College in Oregon, Everytown for Gun Safety unveiled a proposal for new legislation that would clarify the definition of the term "gun dealer" in order to expand federal background checks to cover private gun sales. When critics claimed that the law would not prevent other mass shootings, Everytown research director Ted Alcorn responded by saying that "If the threshold for being a 'good' policy is whether it prevents all future gun violence in America, we will never take another step toward making our communities safer, because there is no single solution to this epidemic" (Farhi 2015).

As Bloomberg gained prominence as a gun control advocate, his positions often put him in direct opposition to the National Rifle Association (NRA) and other gun rights groups. In 2017, when the NRA promoted a measure that would make it easier for gun owners to carry concealed weapons across state lines, Bloomberg announced that he would spend $25 million to fight it. Conservative critics charged that Bloomberg and Everytown exaggerated the prevalence of school shootings in order to generate public outrage and increase support for their cause. When Everytown released a statistic claiming that 74 school shootings had occurred in the 18 months after Sandy Hook, critics noted that the organization counted any incident in which a firearm was discharged in a school or on school grounds, including accidental shootings, suicides, and robberies. "There is an ocean of difference between Sandy Hook, Virginia Tech, and Columbine and a depressed student who (commits suicide) at school, or an accidental discharge," said former Federal Bureau of Investigation behavioral analyst Mark Safarik. "To call them all school shootings may be true in a technical sense but is quite disingenuous on an emotional level" (Carroll 2014).

In 2018, after another mass shooting claimed the lives of 17 people at Marjory Stoneman Douglas High School in Parkland, Florida, Everytown for Gun Safety helped student survivors organize the March for Our Lives, a demonstration in Washington, D.C., and 800 other locations in the United States and around the world to demand action on gun control. Bloomberg's organization donated over $1 million to support and promote the march. Everytown for Gun Safety also launched a new initiative after the Parkland shooting called Students Demand Action to give high school and college students an opportunity to lead the movement to prevent gun violence.

Further Reading

Bloomberg, Michael. 1997. *Bloomberg by Bloomberg.* New York: Wiley.
Bloomberg, Michael. 2012. "Six Ways to Stop Gun Madness: Steps Obama Should Take to Make Real Changes. Our Kids Deserve It." *USA Today,* December 18, 2012. https://www.usatoday.com/story/opinion/2012/12/18/michael-bloomberg-on-need-to-control-guns/1777889/.
Blumberg, Yoni. 2017. "Billionaire Mike Bloomberg Offers to 'Match Every Donation' to Fight Gun Violence." CNBC, October 4, 2017. https://www.cnbc.com/2017/10/04/mike-bloomberg-offers-to-match-every-donation-to-fight-gun-violence.html.
Brennan, Margaret. 2018. "'There's No Leadership on Gun Reform' Says Michael Bloomberg." CBS News, April 20, 2018. https://www.cbsnews.com/news/theres-no-leadership-on-gun-reform-says-michael-bloomberg/.
Carroll, Lauren. 2014. "Have There Been 74 School Shootings since Sandy Hook? A Closer Look at a Tricky Statistic." Politifact, June 13, 2014. https://www.politifact.com/truth-o-meter/statements/2014/jun/13/everytown-gun-safety/have-there-been-74-school-shootings-sandy-hook-clo/.
Farhi, Arden, and Stephanie Condon. 2015. "Bloomberg Backed Group Presents Gun Safety Proposal to White House." CBS News, November 12, 2015. https://www.cbsnews.com/news/bloomberg-backed-group-to-present-gun-proposal-to-white-house/.
Weigel, David, and Wesley Lowery. 2018. "Students Take Charge of Gun-Safety Movement with Some Help from Existing Groups." *Washington Post,* February 21, 2018. https://www.washingtonpost.com/powerpost/students-take-charge-of-gun-safety-movement-with-some-help-from-existing-groups/2018/02/20/eeeb8c58-166d-11e8-92c9-376b4fe57ff7_story.html?utm_term=.0d28d70e602d.

Jaclyn Corin (2000–)

Parkland school shooting survivor and March for Our Lives organizer

Jaclyn Corin was born on October 27, 2000, and grew up in Parkland, Florida. She had a passion for ballet throughout her youth and took dance classes for more than a dozen years. Corin attended Marjory Stoneman Douglas (MSD) High School, where she served as class president during both her freshman and junior years. On February 14, 2018, Corin's student leadership responsibilities included delivering carnations to students in Building 12 for Valentine's Day. A few minutes after she finished, a former MSD student armed with a semiautomatic rifle entered the building, pulled a fire alarm, and began shooting students and teachers as they emerged from classrooms. The perpetrator killed 17 students and staff members, including Corin's close friend Joaquin Oliver and a girl who had just received a carnation.

During the incident and its aftermath, Corin spent two hours hiding in a locked classroom full of terrified students until a SWAT team arrived to free them. Given the frequency of mass shootings in twenty-first-century America, MSD students were raised to consider active-shooter drills part of their normal routine. As a result, the experience seemed sadly familiar to Corin. "Literally when I was in the room hiding, I wasn't even that surprised that this was happening," she related. "That sounds terrifying to say, but it's true. I was like, 'I'm not utterly shocked that this is happening at my school because it's so common these days.' It breaks my heart to have to think like that. No one should have to expect something to happen to them" (Sheppard 2018).

For Corin, feelings of shock and grief quickly turned into anger and determination to take action to prevent future school shootings. "It seemed like there was something in me that was telling me I had to do something about it. I couldn't just sit back and watch this happen over and over again," she noted. "That's what I'd always done—until the faces on the news became faces that I recognized. That's when I knew it was time to step up" (Sheppard 2018). Corin began posting her feelings on social media the night of the shooting, and some of her words reached the ears of Debbie Wasserman Schultz, a member of the U.S. House of Representatives from Florida and former chair of the Democratic National Committee. Schultz recommended that Corin contact Florida senator Lauren Book to arrange a visit by MSD students to the state capital. "I was terrified," Corin recalled. "I'm a 17-year-old calling a Florida state senator. That's just not normal" (Cullen 2018).

With assistance from the legislators, Corin organized an eight-hour bus trip to Tallahassee for 100 MSD students and 15 adult chaperones to advocate for gun control legislation. She arranged for buses, meals, lodging, and meetings with lawmakers, and she collected permission slips from parents. Corin recognized that it was important to act as quickly as possible to take advantage of the national media attention swirling around her school and community. "The news forgets," she noted. "Very quickly. And if we were all talk and no action, people wouldn't take us as seriously. We needed a critical mass event" (Cullen 2018). A few weeks after their visit the Florida legislature passed its first major gun control law in 20 years, the MSD High School Public Safety Act. Although the law did not address all of the students' concerns, it increased the minimum age for firearm purchases from 18 to 21, established mandatory waiting periods and criminal background checks, and prohibited people deemed mentally unstable or potentially violent from purchasing guns.

Corin also cofounded the political action group Never Again MSD with her classmate Cameron Kasky and several other students. The group launched a social media campaign using the hashtag #NeverAgain and sponsored the National School Walkout on March 14. "Parkland became the epicenter of the long-standing gun violence issue after the massacre. *Everyone* was listening," Corin recalled. "We wasted no time trying to make change happen. My hometown now had the platform to speak for the people that have long been silenced, and together, we used our voices—in interviews, social media campaigns, and town halls—in our fight to make a difference" (Corin 2018). Corin was featured on the cover of *Time* magazine, appeared on television with Rachel Maddow and Ellen DeGeneres, and created a YouTube video called *What If* that received nearly 1.5 million views in a matter of days.

On March 24 Corin and her fellow activists spoke at the March for Our Lives, a national student-led demonstration against gun violence that attracted an estimated 800,000 people to Washington, D.C., and a total of 2 million protesters in 800 other locations in the United States and around the world. Corin and other organizers received praise for featuring the voices of students of color in the March for Our Lives. The MSD students recognized that the school shooting in Parkland attracted media attention because it happened in an affluent area, whereas young people from underprivileged backgrounds faced much greater risks of becoming victims of gun violence. "I realized that my classmates and I needed to fight, not only for us, but for those who experience gun violence on *every* level," Corin stated. "This is a shared stage—we're giving people who have to deal with this every day the chance to be heard and bring about change" (Corin 2018).

During the summer of 2018, Corin and other Never Again activists took part in a cross-country bus tour to encourage young people to register to vote. They contended that making gun control a voting issue would reduce the political influence of the National Rifle Association and facilitate the reform of gun laws. Corin argued that her generation had the power to make lasting changes to prevent future school shootings. "*Never live your life with the idea that you're only one person and your voice doesn't matter,*" she stated. "One voice can make a huge difference, there is strength in numbers, and that's what the March for Our Lives is all about. Young people will change the world (soon enough), so when we're the adults, our own children can grow up in a world where they feel safe and worry-free" (Corin 2018).

Further Reading

Corin, Jaclyn. 2018. "I Helped Organize the March for Our Lives Because There Is Strength in Numbers." *Seventeen,* March 21, 2018. https://www.seven teen.com/life/real-girl-stories/a19480107/jaclyn-corin-march-for -our-lives-protest-gun-control/.

Cullen, Dave. 2018. "'The News Forgets. Very Quickly.' Inside the Marjory Stoneman Douglas Students' Incredible Race to Make History." *Vanity Fair,* March 7, 2018. https://www.vanityfair.com/news/2018/03/inside-the -marjory-stoneman-douglas-students-race-to-make-history.

Sheppard, Elena. 2018. "Jaclyn Corin Wasn't 'Utterly Shocked' by the Parkland Shooting, and That Sad Fact Has Inspired Her Generation to Speak Out." Yahoo! News, May 29, 2018. https://www.yahoo.com/lifestyle/jaclyn -corin-wasnt-utterly-shocked-parkland-shooting-sad-fact-inspired-gen eration-speak-235731846.html.

Witt, Emily. 2018. "How the Survivors of Parkland Began the Never Again Movement." *New Yorker,* February 19, 2018. https://www.newyorker.com /news/news-desk/how-the-survivors-of-parkland-began-the-never-again -movement.

Gabby Giffords (1970–)

Former U.S. representative from Arizona, gun violence victim, and gun safety advocate

Gabrielle Dee Giffords was born in Tucson, Arizona, on June 8, 1970. Her father, Spencer Giffords, ran a tire and auto service company, and her mother, Gloria Fraser Giffords, was an art historian. Giffords was an active and adventurous girl who grew up riding both horses and motorcycles. After graduating from University High School in Tucson, she earned a bachelor's degree from Scripps College—a small all-female school in California— in 1993. Giffords spent a year in Chihuahua, Mexico, on a Fulbright scholarship before continuing her education at Cornell University, earning a master's degree in regional planning in 1996. She then returned to Tucson to become president of her family's business, the El Campo Tire Warehouse chain.

In 2000, Giffords sold the company to Goodyear Tire and launched a successful campaign for a seat in the Arizona House of Representatives. Two years later, she became the youngest woman ever elected to the Arizona Senate. She won reelection in 2004 but resigned her seat the following year to campaign to represent Arizona's Eighth District in the U.S. House of Representatives. Although she ran as a Democrat in a previously Republican district, Giffords won the election with 54 percent of the vote. As a member of Congress, she built a reputation as a political moderate who adopted a bipartisan approach toward many issues. Some of her key legislative interests included immigration, health care, education, and the environment.

In 2007, Giffords married Captain Mark Kelly, a decorated U.S. Navy pilot and astronaut who took part in four NASA space shuttle missions. They established a commuter marriage, with Giffords dividing her time between Washington, D.C., and Arizona and Kelly living primarily in Houston, Texas. Their family also included Kelly's teenage daughters from his first marriage, Claudia and Claire.

Giffords won reelection in both 2008 and 2010. On January 8, 2011, shortly after beginning her third term in office, she attended an event called "Congress on Your Corner" in the parking lot of a Safeway supermarket in suburban Tucson. While Giffords met with constituents, 22-year-old Jared Lee Loughner pulled out a gun and shot her through the head at close range. The shooter then opened fire on the crowd of people surrounding Giffords. He killed 6 people, including U.S. district court judge John Roll, and wounded 13 others before bystanders managed to subdue him. Investigators later learned that the shooter had developed a fixation on Giffords and intentionally targeted her in an assassination attempt. He was eventually charged with murder and sentenced to life in prison.

Although early news reports erroneously claimed that Giffords had been killed, she survived the shooting with the help of a member of her staff, Daniel Hernandez, who immediately provided first aid at the scene. She was rushed to University Medical Center in Tucson in critical condition and underwent emergency brain surgery. "Ninety percent of people who suffer that kind of wound don't survive," Kelly stated, "and the ones that do typically never get out of bed again" (McCleary 2017). Giffords defied the odds and began a slow but steady recovery. By the end of January, doctors had removed her breathing tube, upgraded her condition to good, and transferred her to the Texas Institute for Rehabilitation and

Research at Memorial Hermann Medical Center in Houston. By May, Giffords regained use of her left side and began taking steps. Her doctors allowed her to travel to the Kennedy Space Center in Florida to watch the launch of the space shuttle *Endeavor*, with her husband on board as commander.

Over the next six months, Giffords was discharged from the hospital, gave an interview to ABC News, and cowrote a memoir with her husband titled *Gabby: A Story of Courage and Hope*. She continued to experience physical effects of her brain injury, including partial paralysis on the right side of her body, limited peripheral vision, and difficulty speaking. "To communicate basic ideas might take 20 times as long as it used to," Kelly noted. "It requires a lot of patience" (McCleary 2017). In January 2012, Giffords resigned from Congress to focus on rehabilitation. Her former aide Ron Barber, who was also injured in the Tucson shooting, won a special election to finish her term. Throughout her recovery, Giffords inspired many people with her positive attitude and courage. "The injury Gabby suffered was horrific," her husband acknowledged. "It will affect her the rest of her life. If roles were reversed, I'd be a little bit bitter, but she isn't. She pops up every day looking ahead and trying to figure out how to be a positive force in the world" (McCleary 2017).

In January 2013, a month after a mass shooting took the lives of 26 people at Sandy Hook Elementary School in Connecticut, Giffords and Kelly launched Americans for Responsible Solutions, a nonprofit organization aimed at promoting gun safety and preventing gun violence. Giffords approached the issue from the perspective of someone supportive of gun ownership rights. "Mark and I are gun owners. When we launched our organization, we wanted to prove that it's possible to stand up for the Second Amendment while also standing up for stronger gun laws that keep us safe," she noted. "Every day, almost 100 Americans—toddlers, kids, and adults—die from a gunshot. In no other developed country do leaders allow so many citizens to die from this preventable epidemic. We must never accept this level of gun violence in America as normal. We must keep building momentum to save more lives in the years to come" (Giffords 2018). Giffords appeared before the Senate Judiciary Committee to demand action on gun violence.

In 2016, Americans for Responsible Solutions joined forces with the Law Center to Prevent Gun Violence, and the new organization became known as Giffords. The group advocated for laws requiring background checks on all gun purchases and against laws allowing people to carry guns in public without permits or training. The group also worked to elect leaders who supported meaningful measures to prevent gun violence.

"Heading into 2018, candidates across the country recognize that gun safety is at the forefront of voters' minds, and a record number are expected to make gun violence prevention a part of their platform," Giffords stated. "If you're frustrated by the fact that your leaders have yet to do anything to address gun violence, don't forget that you get the final word. After all, there's only one remedy for a Congress that won't take action to keep us safe: a Congress that can" (Giffords 2018).

In 2017, the U.S. Navy honored Giffords's career in public service by commissioning a new combat ship as the USS *Gabrielle Giffords*. She became only the third living woman to have an American warship named after her and the first since First Lady Martha Washington in 1776.

Further Reading

Giffords: Courage to Prevent Gun Violence. https://giffords.org/.

Giffords, Gabrielle. 2018. "Getting Shot Seven Years Ago Gave Me Courage to Fight Gun Violence." *USA Today,* January 8, 2018. https://www.usatoday.com/story/opinion/2018/01/08/seven-years-after-being-shot-were-still-standing-up-gun-lobby-gabby-giffords-column/1011400001/.

Giffords, Gabrielle, and Mark Kelly. 2014. *Enough: Our Fight to Keep America Safe from Gun Violence.* New York: Scribner.

Giffords, Gabrielle, Mark Kelly, and Jeffrey Zaslow. 2011. *Gabby: A Story of Courage and Hope.* New York: Scribner.

McCleary, Kathleen. 2017. "Life Is Good: The Story of Mark Kelly and Gabby Giffords." *Parade,* February 10, 2017. https://parade.com/545964/kmccleary/life-is-good-the-story-of-mark-kelly-and-gabby-giffords/.

Emma González (1999–)

Parkland school shooting survivor and gun control advocate

Emma González was born on November 11, 1999, in Parkland, Florida. She is the youngest of three children born to Beth González, a math tutor, and Jose González, a cybersecurity attorney who immigrated to the United States from Cuba in 1968. González attended Marjory Stoneman Douglas (MSD) High School, where her favorite subjects were creative writing and astronomy. She served as president of the school's Gay-Straight Alliance chapter and also worked on a student project to send a weather balloon to the edge of Earth's atmosphere.

On February 14, 2018, a former MSD student armed with a semiautomatic rifle entered a building on the high school campus, pulled a fire alarm, and began shooting students and teachers as they emerged from classrooms. González hid in the auditorium with other students for two hours until police officers came to release them. Earlier that day, González and her classmates in Advanced Placement U.S. Government had discussed the ways in which special interest groups, such as the Sierra Club and the National Rifle Association (NRA), lobbied government officials and contributed money to election campaigns in order to gain political influence and shape legislation in their favor. In the aftermath of the shooting, González grew angry at politicians who, in her view, prioritized NRA funding over protecting students from gun violence.

On February 17, González expressed her views in a powerful 11-minute speech at a gun control rally in front of the Broward County Courthouse in Fort Lauderdale. "Maybe the adults have gotten used to saying, 'It is what it is,'" she declared, "but if us students have learned anything, it's that if you do not study, you will fail. And in this case, if you actively do nothing, people will continually end up dead. We are going to be the kids you read about in textbooks. Not because we're going to be another statistic about mass shooting in America, but because . . . we are going to be the last mass shooting" (Pearl 2018). She called on young people to rise up in protest and demand meaningful reform of the nation's gun laws.

Toward the end of her speech, González led the crowd in a refrain of "We call BS" in response to a list of reasons commonly proffered for inaction on gun reform. The refrain quickly became a slogan for the student-led movement to end gun violence. "I knew I would get my job done properly at that rally if I got people chanting something," she recalled. "And I thought 'We call BS' has four syllables, that's good, I'll use that. I didn't want to say the actual curse words. . . . This message doesn't need to be thought of in a negative way at all" (Feller 2018). News footage of González's tearful speech went viral online, and she quickly emerged as a leading voice among gun control advocates. "I didn't think it would go viral at all," she admitted. "It went so far and so fast. I've got celebrities tweeting about me" (Pearl 2018). When González established her own Twitter account after the rally, using the handle @Emma4Change, she amassed over 1 million followers in a matter of days.

On February 21, González and fellow MSD student activists participated in a televised CNN town hall meeting with Florida lawmakers, including Republican senator Marco Rubio and Democratic senator Bill Nelson, as well as NRA national spokesperson Dana Loesch. González challenged Loesch to explain her position on the lenient gun laws that allowed the perpetrator of the MSD shooting to purchase an assault weapon, despite the fact that he had previously come to the attention of law enforcement for threatening to harm people. "Dana Loesch, I want you to know that we will support your two children in the way that you will not," González began. "The shooter at our school obtained weapons that he used on us legally. Do you believe that it should be harder to obtain the semiautomatic weapons and the modifications for these weapons to make them fully automatic, like bump stocks?" (Tapper 2018). When Loesch attempted to avoid the question by talking about mental illness, González interrupted her to insist upon receiving an answer. Loesch continued to sidestep, however, and declined to offer her personal opinion.

Beginning a few days after the shooting, González worked with a group of 20 fellow student survivors to launch the Never Again campaign to prevent gun violence. They organized the March for Our Lives, a nationwide student-led demonstration that took place on March 24 in Washington, D.C., and in 800 other locations in the United States and around the world. González delivered one of the most memorable speeches at the D.C. march. After mentioning the names of the 17 people who were murdered at her school and describing things they had loved to do but would no longer be around to experience, she stopped speaking and stood silently with tears streaming down her face. Finally, an alarm on her phone chimed, and González informed the crowd that she had been onstage for six minutes, which was the duration of the Parkland school shooting. "The whole point of that silence was to create an environment where people could be upset, because it was a rough time period," she explained. "And I'm getting emotional talking about it now because I'm remembering that mindset. But it was important to do" (Jamieson 2018).

González's high-profile activism made her a target of right-wing conspiracy theorists and conservative critics. Some claimed that she was not a high school student at all, but a "crisis actor" who was paid to use the media attention surrounding the tragedy to generate support for liberal causes. Others mocked her crewcut hair style, which she said she adopted because it provided relief from the Florida heat, or insulted her bisexual identity. One commentator called her a communist because she wore a Cuban flag patch on the sleeve of her jacket. Supporters pointed out that the flag dated from a time before the Cuban Revolution (1953–1959) brought dictator Fidel Castro to power and had been used by many Cuban Americans to demonstrate respect for their ethnic heritage. Finally, some critics circulated a meme on social media that appeared to show González tearing up a copy of the U.S. Constitution. The image was doctored, however, from a magazine photo shoot in which she tore up a shooting-range target. "We have always been told that if we see something wrong, we need to speak up," González noted. "But now that we are, all we're getting is disrespect from the people who made the rules in the first place. Adults like us when we have strong test scores, but they hate us when we have strong opinions" (González 2018).

After graduating from MSD High School in May 2018, González and other student survivors embarked on a 70-city bus tour across the United States to encourage young people to register to vote. "We're trying to make sure those elected officials that are being supported by the NRA are not elected in the upcoming midterm elections," she explained. "That is one of the strongest mission statements we have right now. We don't want these people in charge of us anymore" (Pearl 2018). When the tour ended, González began her postsecondary education at the New College of Florida. She planned to continue her vocal activism on gun control and other issues, perhaps by pursuing a career in politics. "We are tired of practicing school shooter drills and feeling scared of something we should never have to think about. We are tired of being ignored," she stated. "So we are speaking up for those who don't have anyone listening to them, for those who can't talk about it just yet, and for those who will never speak again. We are grieving, we are furious, and we are using our words fiercely and desperately because that's the only thing standing between us and this happening again" (González 2018).

Further Reading

Feller, Madison. 2018. "Emma González Shares the Story behind Her Moving 'We Call BS' Gun Reform Speech." *Elle*, February 23, 2018. https://www .elle.com/culture/career-politics/a18671363/parkland-students-shoot ing-ellen-degeneres-emma-Gonzalez/.

Gonázlez, Emma. 2018. "Parkland Student Emma González Opens Up about Her Fight for Gun Control." *Harper's Bazaar*, February 26, 2018. https:// www.harpersbazaar.com/culture/politics/a18715714/protesting-nra-gun -control-true-story/.

Jamieson, Amber. 2018. "Emma González Literally Sipped Her Tea When Asked about the NRA Losing Money Because of March for Our Lives." BuzzFeed, August 10, 2018. https://www.buzzfeednews.com/article/amberjamieson /emma-Gonzalez-march-for-our-lives-tour.

Miller, Lisa. 2018. "War Room." New York Magazine, March 5, 2018. http:// nymag.com/intelligencer/2018/03/on-the-ground-with-parkland-teens -as-they-plot-a-revolution.html?gtm=bottom&gtm=bottom.

Pearl, Diana. 2018. "Everything to Know about Emma González, the Florida School Shooting Survivor Fighting to End Gun Violence." *People*, February 23, 2018. https://people.com/crime/everything-to-know-about-emma

-Gonzalez-the-florida-school-shooting-survivor-fighting-for-gun-vio
lence-prevention/.

Tapper, Jake. 2018. "Transcript: Stoneman Students' Questions to Lawmakers
and the NRA at CNN Town Hall." CNN, February 22, 2018. https://
www.cnn.com/2018/02/22/politics/cnn-town-hall-full-video-transcript
/index.html.

Nicole Hockley (1970?–)

Gun violence prevention expert and cofounder of Sandy Hook Promise

Nicole Hockley grew up in Rhode Island and graduated from Cranston
High School East in 1988. After earning a degree in English and theater
from Trinity College in Hartford, Connecticut, she moved to the United
Kingdom, where she completed a student exchange program in 1991. She
married Ian Hockley, a British citizen who worked in information technology, and they settled in Hampshire, England. They eventually had two
sons, Jake and Dylan.

Hockley lived in the United Kingdom for 18 years, working in strategic
marketing and communications for several companies and starting her
family. In 2011, she and her husband decided to move to the United
States. Ian Hockley accepted a position with IBM in New York City, and
the family found a home in the quiet bedroom community of Newtown,
Connecticut. "The schools here have been amazing, and the people in my
neighborhood are incredible," Hockley wrote at the time. "Newtown is a
wonderful place to live and we're looking forward to being here a long,
long time" (Myers 2012).

While her children adjusted to life in a new country, Hockley took time
off work to be a full-time mom. She worked closely with the teachers at
Sandy Hook Elementary School in Newtown to arrange an individualized
education program for her younger son, Dylan, who was diagnosed as
being on the autism spectrum. Dylan successfully integrated into his first-
grade class with the help of a special education aide, Anne Marie Murphy.

On December 14, 2012, a gunman armed with an AR-15 semiautomatic rifle forced his way into Sandy Hook Elementary School and murdered 20 first-grade students and 6 educators. When the shooter entered
Dylan's classroom, Murphy wrapped her arms around the six-year-
old boy to protect him, but they were both killed. Hockley's older son,
Jake, was at Sandy Hook on the day of the shooting. Although he evacu-
ated safely, the experience and the tragic loss of his brother deeply trau-
matized him.

Immediately after the shooting, Hockley and her husband considered moving back to England to escape the specter of gun violence, which claims the lives of nearly 35,000 people each year in the United States (Sandy Hook Promise 2018). They ultimately decided to honor Dylan's memory by working to prevent other parents from experiencing the gun-related death of a child. "We had a choice to either run away to a safer environment to bring up Jake, or do something to change the environment we'd moved to. We decided to try to make it better," she recalled. "At Dylan's funeral, Ian and I looked at each other and both said something needed to be done, and we decided to try to make that change" (Aldridge 2015).

Along with the families of other Sandy Hook shooting victims, Hockley cofounded Sandy Hook Promise (SHP), a nonprofit organization aimed at teaching people about the causes of gun violence and providing them with tools to help prevent it. She served as its director of communications and outreach and emerged as one of its main spokespeople. By 2018, more than 2.5 million supporters had taken the SHP pledge "to do all I can to protect children from gun violence by encouraging and supporting solutions that create safer, healthier homes, schools and communities" (Sandy Hook Promise 2018).

One of SHP's main missions involves training people to recognize common warning signs exhibited by individuals at risk for gun violence and to intervene before they hurt someone. The perpetrator of the Sandy Hook shooting, 20-year-old Adam Lanza, lived with his mother across the street from the Hockley family. Hockley learned from Federal Bureau of Investigation behavioral analysts that many elements of his profile matched those of other school shooters. "Our shooter didn't just snap and go to the school and kill people," she noted. "He had been planning the shooting over a year and there had been lots of signs and signals throughout his life that he was at risk of doing something like this and committing acts of violence and self-harm. I realized that the whole shooting was totally preventable, if only someone had acted on these signs and signals" (Bogard and Hoffman 2017).

When a gunman killed 17 students and staff members at Marjory Stoneman Douglas High School in Parkland, Florida, in February 2018, Hockley struggled with the emotional impact. "Like any person who hears about another mass shooting, there is an absolute gut punch and a heartbreak to know that it's happened again," she acknowledged. "It also just brings us straight back to losing our children and knowing what that feels like, tearing that scab off of your heart all over again. . . . And knowing that these poor families and communities that are impacted, that they have a long and endlessly heartbreaking journey ahead of them" (Bologna 2017). Despite her personal struggles, Hockley immediately flew to Florida to counsel the victims' families.

After meeting with two Parkland survivors who became leaders in the emerging #NeverAgain movement to end gun violence, Cameron Kasky and Sofie Whitney, Hockley expressed confidence that the student activists would carry the momentum forward and achieve meaningful change. "They were elementary school kids when Sandy Hook happened. This is all they've experienced, active shooter drills and school violence and gun violence," she stated. "At this point with Parkland, it's new voices, it's the kids advocating for themselves rather than the adults advocating for them. What parents can listen to a kid say, 'Please protect me, and keep me safe,' and not respond? It's got a different energy now, and social media certainly helps. The kids are brilliant in organizing, but sometimes I think if Sandy Hook hadn't happened, then Parkland would be the beginning instead of being, I hope, the end" (Feller 2018).

Further Reading

Aldridge, Gemma. 2015. "Dylan Hockey: Mum of British Sandy Hook Massacre Victim 'Eaten Up with Guilt Every Day.'" *Mirror*, March 14, 2015. https://www.mirror.co.uk/news/world-news/dylan-hockey-mum-british-sandy-5337230.

Bogard, Ally, and Allie Hoffman. 2017. "On Resilience: This Mom Turned the Pain of Her Son's Shooting into a Multi-Million Dollar Non-Profit." *Forbes*, March 17, 2017. https://www.forbes.com/sites/bogardandhoffman/2017/03/07/on-resilience-this-mom-turned-the-pain-of-her-sons-shooting-into-a-multi-million-dollar-non-profit/#4b727f107ce3.

Bologna, Caroline. 2017. "Six Parents of Sandy Hook Shooting Victims on Moving Forward after Unspeakable Loss." *Huffington Post*, December 14, 2017. https://www.huffingtonpost.com/entry/sandy-hook-victims-5-years_us_5a2ac6cce4b073789f695659.

Feller, Madison. 2018. "Nicole Hockley Lost Her Son at Sandy Hook. Then She Had to Send Her Surviving Son Back to School." *Elle*, March 6, 2018. https://www.elle.com/culture/career-politics/a19053193/sandy-hook-shooting-parkland-gun-safety-president-trump/.

Myers, Russell. 2012. "'The Neighbors Here Are Incredible': How Mother of British Victim Fell in Love with Small Town Now Forever Tainted by Tragedy." *Daily Mail*, December 15, 2012. http://www.dailymail.co.uk/news/article-2248891/Dylan-Hockley-How-mother-British-victim-fell-love-Newtown-Connecticut.html.

Sandy Hook Promise. 2018. https://www.sandyhookpromise.org.

David Hogg (2000–)

Parkland school shooting survivor and gun control advocate

David Miles Hogg was born on April 12, 2000, and grew up in Torrance, California. His father, Kevin Hogg, is a former agent of the Federal Bureau of Investigation (FBI), and his mother, Rebecca Boldrick, is a teacher. David Hogg has a younger sister, Lauren. As a boy, Hogg routinely resisted following rules and doing what his parents wanted him to do, such as taking golf or sailing lessons. "I would just turn everything into an us-versus-them situation," he admitted (Hogg and Hogg 2018). Hogg struggled to learn to read in elementary school until he received a diagnosis of dyslexia in the fourth grade.

During Hogg's freshman year of high school, his father retired from the FBI and the family moved from California to Parkland, Florida. Hogg chose to attend Marjory Stoneman Douglas (MSD) High School because it offered courses in video production that meshed well with his interest in broadcast journalism. He joined the TV-production club, carried a camera around to take pictures of school events, and worked as a TeenLink reporter for the *Sun-Sentinel* newspaper. By the time he was a senior, Hogg had connected with a small group of like-minded friends, including Emma González, Delaney Tarr, and Ryan Deitsch. "We're the misfits," Hogg said. "We're really nihilist. We love making jokes and being self-deprecating" (Miller 2018a).

On February 14, 2018, a former MSD student armed with a semiautomatic rifle entered a building on the high school campus, pulled a fire alarm, and began shooting students and teachers as they emerged from classrooms. Hogg, who was in an Advanced Placement Environmental Science class at that time, recalled hearing popping noises that sounded like gunshots, but he and his classmates assumed it was a drill. When they stepped into the hallway, however, a custodian told them it was a code-red emergency and warned them to take cover. Hogg went into a nearby culinary arts classroom and hid in a locked storeroom with about 60 other students.

While they hid in the darkened room, Hogg pulled out his cell phone and began interviewing his classmates. As an aspiring journalist, he felt a duty to document the experience in case they did not live through it. "I want to show these people exactly what's going on when these children are facing bullets flying through classrooms and students are dying trying to get an education," he explained. "That's not OK, and that's not acceptable, and we need to fix that" (Andone 2018). Hogg and his sister eventually left the school safely and were reunited with their parents. The gunman murdered 17 students and teachers, however, including 4 of Lauren Hogg's friends.

Later that evening, after submitting his cell phone video to the *Sun-Sentinel,* Hogg returned to MSD on his bicycle to report on the aftermath of the tragedy. While he was filming background shots of bullet holes in the school windows, he encountered a television crew from Fox News and offered his eyewitness account of the shooting. Before the interview concluded, Hogg made a passionate plea for the nation's leaders to take action on gun control. "Can I say one more thing to the audience?" he insisted. "I don't want this just to be another mass shooting. I don't want this to be something that people forget" (Miller 2018a). Hogg's poise, command of statistics, and righteous anger on camera led to a slew of interview requests the following day from ABC News, CNN, and MSNBC. "Everybody's getting used to this, and that's not okay," he asserted. "There have been 18 more mass shootings than there need to be this year at schools. It needs to come to an end" (Miller 2018a).

In the days after the shooting, junior Cameron Kasky hosted gatherings of MSD students at his home to organize a response. Hogg and his friends soon joined this group, which launched the #NeverAgain hashtag on social media and planned the March for Our Lives protest in Washington, D.C. Hogg became one of the most visible faces of the Never Again movement, frequently promoting gun control in interviews and speeches and at town hall meetings. "Angry, edgy, righteous, relentless, he was the warrior who would take anyone on and refused to be knocked off message," said a profile in *New York* magazine (Miller 2018a). Hogg quickly attracted more than 800,000 followers on Twitter, where he criticized politicians who accepted campaign money from the National Rifle Association and sought to mobilize young voters to remove them from office.

As a prominent gun control advocate, Hogg became a target for right-wing conspiracy theorists. Various sources claimed that he was not really a student at MSD, that he was not there at the time of the shooting, or that his comments afterward were scripted or coached. Some accused him of being a paid "crisis actor" sent to the scene by powerful liberals intent on undermining the Donald Trump administration or confiscating firearms from law-abiding citizens. Hogg argued that he supported the Second Amendment rights of safe, responsible gun owners and noted that his father carried a service revolver throughout his years with the FBI. Nevertheless, Hogg's outspoken activism attracted hateful comments and death threats on social media. "It's a testament to the sick immaturity and broken state of our government when these people feel the need to peddle conspiracy theories about people that were in a school shooting where

17 people died," he stated. "It's immature, rude, and inhuman for these people to destroy the people trying to prevent the death of the future of America" (Nashrulla and Smidt 2018).

After graduating from MSD in May 2018, Hogg and other Never Again activists embarked on a cross-country bus tour to encourage young people to register to vote and to increase public support for gun control legislation. He also collaborated with his sister to write a best-selling book about the Parkland shooting and its impact on their family and community, *#Never Again: A New Generation Draws the Line*. Although Hogg was accepted to several colleges—and many others, including Harvard University, expressed interest in him after he emerged as a prominent figure in the gun violence prevention movement—he decided to take a year off to campaign for gun sense candidates in the 2018 midterm elections. He hoped to enter college in the fall of 2019, and his future plans include entering politics and running for office. "I think I've come to that conclusion," he explained. "I want to be at least part of the change in Congress" (Miller 2018a).

Further Reading

Andone, Dakin. 2018. "Student Journalist Interviewed Classmates as Shooter Walked Parkland School Halls." CNN, February 18, 2018. https://www.cnn.com/2018/02/17/us/david-hogg-profile-florida-shooting/index.html.

Hogg, David, and Lauren Hogg. 2018. *#Never Again: A New Generation Draws the Line*. New York: Random House.

Miller, Lisa. 2018a. "David Hogg, after Parkland." New York Magazine, August 19, 2018. http://nymag.com/intelligencer/2018/08/david-hogg-is-taking-his-gap-year-at-the-barricades.html.

Miller, Lisa. 2018b. "War Room." New York Magazine, March 5, 2018. http://nymag.com/intelligencer/2018/03/on-the-ground-with-parkland-teens-as-they-plot-a-revolution.html?gtm=bottom&gtm=bottom.

Nashrulla, Tasneem, and Remy Smidt. 2018. "Donald Trump Jr. Liked Tweets Promoting a Conspiracy Theory about a Florida Shooting Survivor." BuzzFeed, February 20, 2018. https://www.buzzfeednews.com/article/tasneemnashrulla/donald-trump-jr-conspiracy-theory-florida-shooting-survivor#.biLOEZ3Qxl.

Cameron Kasky (2000–)

Parkland school shooting survivor and cofounder of Never Again MSD

Cameron Kasky was born on November 11, 2000. His father, Jeff Kasky, is an attorney who assesses the legal risks borne by promoters of concerts, festivals, and other large events. Cameron has a younger brother, Holden, who is on the autism spectrum. Both Kasky boys attended Marjory Stoneman Douglas (MSD) High School in Parkland, Florida. Cameron was known as a class clown and a theater kid who enjoyed performing in the school's dramatic productions. "I'm a talker," he acknowledged. "I never shut up" (Witt 2018).

On February 14, 2018, a former MSD student armed with a semiautomatic rifle entered a building on the high school campus, pulled a fire alarm, and began shooting students and teachers as they emerged from classrooms. Kasky had recently left his drama class to pick up his brother from the special needs classroom. As they began to exit the building, they were told to go back inside and take cover from an active shooter. "It was very confusing, especially since I was surrounded by special needs students," Kasky remembered. "Nobody really knew what was going on. We huddled in a room, listening to terrifying noises we couldn't quite identify, and spent an hour plagued by uncontrolled anxiety . . . waiting for answers. Waiting for somebody to either come in and shoot us or come in and tell us everything was going to be OK" (Kasky 2018).

Members of a SWAT team eventually arrived to free the students. As soon as Kasky returned home safely, his fear turned to anger that the gunman had murdered 17 people at his school with a gun he legally acquired, despite a history of behavioral and mental health issues. Kasky immediately began expressing his outrage on social media. "I'm safe," he wrote on Facebook two hours after the shooting. "Thank you to all the Second Amendment warriors who protected me." Later, in the middle of a sleepless night, Kasky grew determined to find a way to turn the tragedy into action to promote changes to the nation's gun laws. "I just want people to understand what happened and understand that doing nothing will lead to nothing," he posted. "Who'd have thought that concept was so difficult to grasp?" (Witt 2018).

After attending a candlelight vigil for his slain classmates on February 15, Kasky invited his friends Alex Wind and Sofie Whitney to his house to develop a plan to prevent future school shootings. The group stayed up all night launching a gun violence prevention movement on social media using the hashtag #NeverAgain. "Working on a central space that isn't just my personal page for all of us to come together and change this," Kasky wrote (Witt 2018). Over the next few days the group expanded to include around 20 of the most outspoken MSD students, such as Jaclyn Corin, Emma González, David Hogg, and Delaney Tarr. On February 18, the Never Again activists announced plans for the March for Our Lives, a student-led nationwide demonstration against gun violence. "The thing that inspired us to create the march was people saying, 'This is not the time to talk about gun control, this is the time to mourn,'" Kasky noted. "We understand that, so here's the time to talk about gun control. March 24th" (Braca 2018).

On February 21, Kasky and other MSD student activists participated in a CNN town hall meeting with Republican senator Marco Rubio of Florida. Kasky gained prominence in the Never Again movement by confronting Rubio about his willingness to accept campaign contributions from the National Rifle Association (NRA) in the aftermath of the MSD school shooting. "Can you tell me right now that you will not accept a single donation from the NRA in the future?" Kasky demanded. "In the name of 17 people, you cannot ask the NRA to keep their money out of your campaign?" (Caputo and Morin 2018). Although Rubio refused to stop accepting NRA funding, he did shift his stance on raising the minimum age for firearm purchases and restricting the size of ammunition magazines.

In recognition of their gun control advocacy, Kasky and other MSD activists appeared on the cover of *Time* magazine in March. Like other Never Again leaders, however, Kasky frequently became the target of right-wing conspiracy theorists and social media trolls, and he suspended his use of Facebook after receiving death threats. During the summer of 2018, Kasky and fellow student activists embarked on a cross-country bus tour to raise awareness of the problem of gun violence and encourage young people to vote. He found the tour to be an eye-opening experience as far as exposing him to people with different viewpoints and perspectives. "Whenever we're connecting with students who don't necessarily see eye to eye with us, the important thing to keep in mind is empathy, and realizing that we're all human," he said. "As long as we all respect each other, we can move forward with our goals, and try to make as many compromises as possible, and implement as many programs as we can" (Duryea 2018).

When the tour concluded, Kasky decided to leave the March for Our Lives organization he cofounded. He expressed regret about his aggressive questioning of Rubio on television, admitting that his intention was to embarrass the senator rather than to promote constructive dialogue. Kasky also said that he made a mistake by mentioning the MSD shooter's name in interviews and thus giving him the notoriety he sought. Although Kasky felt proud of what he and his friends had accomplished, he wanted to adopt a new approach to resolving political disagreements. "I learned that a lot of our issues politically come from a lack of understanding of other perspectives," he explained. "So often young conservatives and young liberals will go into debate . . . trying to beat the other one as opposed to come to an agreement. I'm working on some efforts to encourage bipartisanship or at least discussion that is productive and help a lot of people avoid the mistakes that I made" (Crane 2018).

Further Reading

Braca, Nina. 2018. "Parkland Students Call for Tighter Gun Control on 'Ellen.'" Billboard, February 23, 2018. https://www.billboard.com/amp/articles /news/8215172/parkland-student-activists-gun-control-ellen-inter view-video.

Caputo, Marc, and Rebecca Morin. 2018. "Facing Jeers and Boos, Rubio Shifts on Guns during Tense Forum." Politico, February 21, 2018. https://www .politico.com/story/2018/02/21/marco-rubio-age-limit-rifles-421647.

Crane, Emily. 2018. "Parkland Shooting Survivor Leaves Gun Control Campaign Group." Daily Mail, September 21, 2018. https://www.dailymail.co.uk /news/article-6193377/March-Lives-founder-Cameron-Kasky-leaves -group.html.

Duryea, Bill. 2018. "We Shined a Light on Just How Rigged the Game Is." Politico, September/October 2018. https://www.politico.com/magazine/story /2018/09/04/parkland-teens-marjory-stoneman-douglas-survivors-inter view-219621.

Harris, Chris. 2018. "What to Know about Cameron Kasky, School Shooting Survivor Allegedly Getting Death Threats from NRA Supporters." *People*, February 26, 2018. https://people.com/crime/cameron-kasky-everything -to-know-parkland-shooting-survivor/.

Kasky, Cameron. 2018. "Parkland Student: My Generation Won't Stand for This." CNN, February 20, 2018. https://www.cnn.com/2018/02/15/opinions /florida-shooting-no-more-opinion-kasky/index.html.

Witt, Emily. 2018. "How the Survivors of Parkland Began the Never Again Movement." *New Yorker,* February 19, 2018. https://www.newyorker.com /news/news-desk/how-the-survivors-of-parkland-began-the-never-again -movement.

Wayne LaPierre (1949–)

Gun rights activist and chief executive officer of the National Rifle Association

Wayne Robert LaPierre Jr. was born on November 8, 1949, in Schenectady, New York. He was the first child born to Hazel and Wayne LaPierre Sr., an accountant. LaPierre Jr. moved with his family to Roanoke, Virginia, when he was five years old. After earning a master's degree in government from Boston College, he briefly served as an aide to Vic Thomas, a Democrat who represented Roanoke in the Virginia House of Delegates. In 1977

LaPierre joined the National Rifle Association (NRA) as a lobbyist, initially serving as a liaison between the state government and the NRA's Institute for Legislative Action. He rose through the ranks of the organization to become its chief executive officer in 1986 and executive vice president in 1991.

As head of the NRA, LaPierre became one of the leading voices in the contentious national debate over gun rights. In 2013, *Time* magazine placed him among the top 100 most influential people in the world. During his tenure, he modernized the gun rights organization's operations and oversaw tremendous growth in its membership and political power. "The NRA was run like an old-time club when I took over," LaPierre recalled. "We were in the red and getting cut off from our membership" (Markon 2012). Over the next two decades, the NRA spent more than $100 million on political activities and expanded its base of support to include more than 4 million members.

LaPierre became known for his staunch, absolutist interpretation of the Second Amendment. "We must declare that there are no shades of gray in American freedom. It's black and white, all or nothing," he told NRA members at a 2002 annual meeting. "You're with us or against us" (Achenbach, Higham, and Horwitz 2013). LaPierre often contended that liberals sought to abolish the Second Amendment and confiscate guns from law-abiding citizens. Whenever political opponents proposed gun control legislation, he rallied NRA members by warning that the government was "coming for your guns" ("Wayne LaPierre" 2016). LaPierre outlined his philosophy and goals in numerous speeches and books, including *The Global War on Guns: Inside the UN Plan to Destroy the Bill of Rights* (2006) and *The Essential Second Amendment Guide* (2007).

In the mid-1990s LaPierre led opposition to the Brady Bill, which imposed a seven-day waiting period and criminal background checks for gun purchases, and a related federal initiative aimed at banning assault weapons. In a fund-raising letter LaPierre sent to NRA members, he asserted that the federal assault weapons ban "gives jackbooted government thugs more power to take away our constitutional rights, break in our doors, seize our guns, destroy our property and even injure and kill us" (Achenbach, Higham, and Horwitz 2013). Critics charged that LaPierre's words generated fear and incited violence toward government employees and law enforcement personnel. His hard-line approach caused such moderate NRA members as former president George H. W. Bush to withdraw their support for the gun rights lobbying group.

LaPierre's antigovernment rhetoric ignited controversy in 1995, after domestic terrorist Timothy McVeigh bombed a federal office building in Oklahoma City, killing 168 people. Although McVeigh was not associated with the NRA, media attention focused on LaPierre's characterization of federal agents as "jackbooted thugs." LaPierre responded to the criticism by issuing a public apology, but this decision cost him the support of some militant NRA members, who viewed it as a sign of weakness. From that time on, LaPierre stood by his extreme statements despite public outcry or political pressure.

The late 1990s and early 2000s saw some of the most devastating mass shootings in modern history. Several tragic incidents occurred at schools, including Columbine High School in Colorado in 1999, Virginia Tech University in 2007, and Sandy Hook Elementary School in Newtown, Connecticut, in 2012. Following each of these shootings, LaPierre insisted that limiting the availability of guns would not prevent gun violence, declaring that "the only thing that stops a bad guy with a gun is a good guy with a gun" (Achenbach, Higham, and Horwitz 2013). "Is the press and the political class here in Washington, D.C., so consumed by fear and hatred of the NRA and American gun owners," LaPierre said, "that you're willing to accept the world, where real resistance to evil monsters is [an] alone, unarmed school principal left to surrender her life, her life, to shield those children in her care?" (Markon 2012).

In February 2017, another school shooting took the lives of 17 students and faculty members at Marjory Stoneman Douglas High School in Parkland, Florida. The survivors of the school shooting in Parkland launched a national social media campaign, #NeverAgain, aimed at preventing gun violence in schools. They also criticized the influence of the NRA on the American political system as well as the organization's resistance to passing commonsense gun regulations.

LaPierre accused the student activists and their political allies of exploiting the tragedy to pursue stricter gun laws. Instead, he advocated for armed guards at every school in the United States and said the NRA would provide free help to schools that wanted to increase their security. "Demand what works," he said. "Put armed security in every school. Fix the broken mental health system. Enforce the federal gun laws against every criminal thug on the street. Prosecute dangerous people when they show up to buy a gun. And, for God's sake, put every prohibited person into the system. That's what common-sense gun laws look like" (Sherfinski 2018).

Further Reading

Achenbach, Joel, Scott Higham, and Sari Horwitz. 2013. "How NRA's True Believers Converted a Marksmanship Group into a Mighty Gun Lobby." *Washington Post*, January 12, 2013. https://www.washingtonpost.com

/politics/how-nras-true-believers-converted-a-marksmanship-group
-into-a-mighty-gun-lobby/2013/01/12/51c62288–59b9–11e2–88d0
-c4cf65c3ad15_story.html?utm_term=.554a08952ea6.

Markon, Jerry. 2012. "NRA's Wayne LaPierre: The Force behind the Nation's Gun Lobby." *Washington Post,* December 21, 2012. https://www.washing tonpost.com/politics/nras-lapierre-the-force-behind-the-nations-gun -lobby/2012/12/21/599e8b96–4b98–11e2-a6a6-aabac85e8036_story .html?noredirect=on&utm_term=.5d42710fe271.

Sherfinski, David. 2018. "NRA Offers Help to Schools That Hire Armed Guards, Warns of Overreach." *Washington Times,* February 22, 2018. https://www .washingtontimes.com/news/2018/feb/22/wayne-lapierre-nra-ceo-cpac -calls-more-armed-secur/.

"Wayne LaPierre: Executive Vice President and CEO." 2016. NRA on the Record: A Customizable Database of Quotes from the Leaders of the National Rifle Association. http://nraontherecord.org/wayne-lapierre/.

Dana Loesch (1978–)

Conservative talk show host and national spokesperson for the National Rifle Association

Dana Loesch was born Dana Eaton on September 28, 1978, in Hematite, Missouri. She was raised in a blue-collar Democratic family. After her parents divorced when she was five years old, she lived with her single mother in an urban neighborhood that experienced problems with drugs and violence. Loesch found refuge at her grandparents' house in the country, where she spent summers learning to shoot BB guns in the backyard. After graduating from Fox High School in Arnold, Missouri, Loesch enrolled at St. Louis Community College at Meramec. She later transferred to Webster University, where she majored in journalism.

Loesch became involved in politics during her college years, when she supported Democrat Bill Clinton's 1996 presidential campaign. She grew disgruntled with Clinton when his affair with a White House intern resulted in his impeachment, however, and Loesch's political views shifted further following her marriage to a conservative music producer, Chris Loesch, in 2000. After the terrorist attacks against the United States on September 11, 2001, Dana Loesch formally left the Democratic Party and joined the Republican Party, which she felt placed a stronger emphasis on combating terrorism and promoting national security.

Loesch launched her career as a commentator while homeschooling her two children, Ewan and Liam, by writing a blog called "Mamalogues." Her blog attracted so many readers that she turned into a column for the

St. Louis Post-Dispatch newspaper. In 2008 Loesch started discussing politics and current events on her own nationally syndicated radio show, *The Dana Show: The Conservative Alternative.* In 2010 she became editor in chief of the conservative website Big Journalism. Loesch bolstered her credentials as a political analyst by covering the 2012 midterm elections for CNN. The network ended its relationship with her, however, over controversial comments she made in support of U.S. marines who urinated on the corpses of dead Taliban fighters in Afghanistan. In 2013 Loesch hosted the Conservative Political Action Conference, and the following year she launched her own television show, *Dana,* on the Blaze conservative news network.

Loesch emerged as a defender of individual gun ownership in 2014 with the publication of her book *Hands Off My Gun: Defeating the Plot to Disarm America.* The book expressed her opinion that law-abiding American citizens had a fundamental right to own and carry guns for self-protection, and Loesch portrayed efforts to restrict gun access or ownership as a threat to these rights. In 2016, National Rifle Association (NRA) executive vice president Wayne LaPierre invited Loesch to serve as a special adviser on women's policy for the influential gun rights lobbying organization. The following year, she became the national spokesperson for the NRA. "I've been impressed with Dana's command of the issues facing the NRA," LaPierre stated, "as well as her ability to communicate our positions and connect with women, and men, on those issues" (Friedman 2018).

Shortly after becoming the NRA spokesperson, Loesch appeared in a controversial online advertisement aimed at recruiting new members for the organization. Against a backdrop of video footage from Black Lives Matter protests and the Women's March, Loesch claimed that progressive activists "scream racism and sexism and xenophobia and homophobia and smash windows, burn cars, shut down interstates and airports, bully and terrorize the law abiding." She warned gun owners that "the only way we stop this, the only way we save our country and our freedom is to fight this violence of lies with the clenched fist of truth" (Friedman 2018). Critics denounced the ad, describing it as "irresponsible and dangerous propaganda" and "an open call to violence to protect white supremacy" (Holson 2018), and launched a petition demanding its removal.

In February 2018, a mass shooting at Marjory Stoneman Douglas High School in Parkland, Florida, took the lives of 17 students and faculty members. Survivors of the shooting launched the #NeverAgain movement on social media to reform gun laws and promote school safety. The Parkland student activists criticized the influence of the NRA on the American political system as well as the organization's resistance to passing commonsense gun regulations. Loesch rejected the assertion that stricter gun control measures could have prevented the tragedy. Instead, she argued that the Federal Bureau of Investigation and the local police department should have recognized warning signs in the perpetrator's behavior. "That firearm did not walk itself into the school, an individual who was allowed to go unchecked by the Broward County Sheriff's office allowed that firearm to go in this school," she stated. "If someone is online, using their name, saying they're going to shoot up a school, if they're banned from school because they've taken bullets and knives in their backpack to school, if they've been sending messages saying that they're going to shoot and kill their classmates, that, to me, sounds like a potential school shooter" (Wolfgang 2018).

In the aftermath of the Parkland school shooting, Loesch participated in a CNN town hall discussion about gun violence prevention with student activists, parents of victims, and law enforcement officials. Emma González, a Parkland survivor and gun control advocate, repeatedly challenged Loesch to state her position on whether it should be harder to obtain semiautomatic weapons. Loesch avoided the question but generally argued that the regulations proposed by Never Again activists—such as banning assault weapons and increasing the minimum age for gun purchases—would not resolve the issue. A few days later, Loesch drew criticism for appearing insensitive by attacking the media attention surrounding the Parkland shooting and the Never Again movement. "Many in the legacy media love mass shootings," she stated. "I'm not saying that you love the tragedy, but you love the ratings. Crying white mothers are ratings gold" (Freidman 2018).

While Loesch's outspoken defense of gun rights made her a hero to many NRA members, her controversial statements also generated outrage among gun control advocates. Loesch claimed on Twitter that she and her family had to move out of their home because of repeated death threats. "I'm not sad, just determined," she wrote. "Maybe someday people will drop the ideological boundaries and not cherry-pick concern" (Chavez 2018). Despite the animosity she has faced, Loesch remains deeply committed to the NRA and its priorities. "I've been told I'm a whore for the NRA," she noted. "But I believe so strongly in the natural right to bear arms. I feel so passionately about that. . . . I am doing what I want to do, and what I feel fulfilled in doing" (Holson 2018).

Further Reading

Chavez, Nicole. 2018. "Who Is NRA Spokesperson Dana Loesch?" CNN, February 22, 2018. https://www.cnn.com/2018/02/21/us/nra-dana-loesch-profile/index.html.

Friedman, Megan. 2018. "What You Should Know about NRA Spokesperson Dana Loesch." *Esquire,* February 22, 2018. https://www.esquire.com/news -politics/a18663982/who-is-dana-loesch-nra-spokesperson/.

Hawkins, Derek. 2018. "Dana Loesch, the NRA's Brash Spokesperson, Dials Back the Rage at CNN Town Hall." *Washington Post,* February 22, 2018. https:// www.washingtonpost.com/news/morning-mix/wp/2018/02/22/dana -loesch-the-nras-brash-spokeswoman-dials-back-the-rage-at-cnn-town -hall/?utm_term=.71ffa39c8518.

Holson, Laura. 2018. "The National Rifle Association's Telegenic Warrior." *New York Times,* January 20, 2018. https://www.nytimes.com/2018/01/20/style /dana-loesch-national-rifle-association.html.

Wolfgang, Ben. 2018. "NRA Blames FBI, Sheriff's Office for Failing to Prevent Parkland Shooting." *Washington Times,* February 25, 2018. https://www .washingtontimes.com/news/2018/feb/25/dana-loesch-nra-spokes woman-blames-fbi-sheriffs-of/.

Shannon Watts (1971–)

Gun control activist and founder of Moms Demand Action for Gun Sense in America

Shannon Watts was born on January 1, 1971. After earning a degree from the University of Missouri at Columbia in 1994, she spent four years working in public affairs for the Missouri state government. Watts then moved into the private sector and served as a corporate communications director and public relations executive for several large companies, including WellPoint and Monsanto. While she built her career, Watts also married, had two daughters and a son, and divorced. In 2008, she left her corporate job to become a stay-at-home mother and part-time public relations consultant. Around this time she married her second husband, health care executive John Watts Jr., and her family expanded to include two stepdaughters. They settled in Zionsville, a suburb of Indianapolis, Indiana.

Watts did not give much thought to the problem of gun violence until the summer of 2012, when a gunman opened fire in a crowded movie theater in Aurora, Colorado, killing 12 people and injuring 58 others. The next day her young son went to see *The Dark Knight Rises*—the same movie that had been playing in Aurora—and had a panic attack because he thought a person sitting near him had a gun. Six months later, when a mass shooting at Sandy Hook Elementary School in Newtown, Connecticut, took the lives of 26 first-grade students and educators, Watts worried that the tragedy would make her son afraid to go to school. Instead, he seemed resigned to the commonplace occurrence of gun violence in the United States—a reaction that Watts found even more alarming.

Other than donating money to a few Democratic candidates and progressive causes, Watts had not been politically active before the Sandy Hook shooting. In its aftermath, however, she grew determined to do something to help prevent gun violence. She created a Facebook group called One Million Moms for Gun Control that invited mothers across the country to express their anger and frustration and discuss ways to ensure the safety of their children. The group quickly attracted thousands of members and grew into a grassroots movement modeled after Mothers Against Drunk Driving. Watts turned the online group into a nonprofit organization called Moms Demand Action for Gun Sense in America, which eventually included 80 local chapters in all 50 states, and emerged as its national spokesperson. "To go from a stay-at-home mom to a full-time activist traveling the country to talk about gun safety was something I never imagined I'd be doing," Watts acknowledged. "That said, I think my experience in communications, branding, and messaging helped Moms Demand Action become so visible so quickly" (Woo 2018).

Watts and other activists with Moms Demand Action sought to counteract the influence that powerful gun rights groups, such as the National Rifle Association (NRA), held over U.S. gun policy. "I assumed lawmakers were looking out for the safety of my family and community," Watts noted. "As I researched what was causing our nation's gun violence crisis, I learned I was wrong. Too many lawmakers are in the pocket of the National Rifle Association, pushing through their dangerous vision for America: Guns for anyone, anywhere, anytime—no questions asked" (Watts 2016). After the school shooting in Newtown, NRA lobbyists helped defeat legislation aimed at restoring a federal ban on semiautomatic assault weapons and large-capacity ammunition magazines. Rather than reforming gun laws, NRA leaders suggested placing armed security guards in American schools to protect students. "The NRA outlined how they saw the vision of America," Watts stated. "That future is everyone is armed and the bad guys shoot it out with the good guys over our children's heads. That's not tenable" (Barron 2013).

In December 2013, Moms Demand Action combined forces with Mayors Against Illegal Guns, an organization formed and funded by New York City mayor Michael Bloomberg, to create Everytown for Gun Safety. With 5 million supporters, Everytown became the largest group in the gun violence prevention movement. Moms Demand Action served as the center of grassroots activism within Everytown, mobilizing 300,000 volunteers across the country to call and e-mail lawmakers, attend hearings on proposed legislation, organize marches and rallies, and work to elect political candidates who support commonsense gun laws. Moms Demand

Action activists helped defeat hundreds of state and local bills that they believe would have jeopardized the safety of families, including some that would have allowed gun owners to carry weapons in public schools, on college campuses, and without permits or training. The group also promoted legislation aimed at requiring background checks for all gun sales, preventing domestic abusers from buying guns, and funding federal research on gun violence. Finally, Moms Demand Action launched social media campaigns that convinced several national retail and restaurant chains—including Starbucks, Chipotle, and Target—to prohibit customers from bringing guns into their stores.

As Watts gained national recognition for her efforts, she became a target for gun rights supporters hoping to discredit her. An NRA publication questioned her characterization of herself as an apolitical stay-at-home mom who suddenly became concerned about gun violence, and instead portrayed her as a highly paid public relations (PR) professional employed by the liberal antigun billionaire Michael Bloomberg. Watts argued that NRA extremists should not be allowed to define her. "I disagree with this idea that I'm not a regular person," she stated. "They want me to be some kind of PR master. I was a stay-at-home mom in the Midwest who was angry, like millions of other moms" (Wemple 2016).

In February 2018, a mass shooting at Marjory Stoneman Douglas High School in Parkland, Florida, resulted in the deaths of 17 students and staff members. Survivors of the shooting and other high school and college activists joined forces with Moms Demand Action and Everytown to form Students Demand Action for Gun Sense in America. The student-led movement resulted in an increase in membership and donations for all three organizations. Watts expressed determination to build on the momentum to prevent future tragedies. "From suicides to domestic violence shootings to the shootings of law enforcement to shootings motivated by hate or racism, we are fighting to protect our nation's most vulnerable," she declared. "American moms are more powerful and influential in this fight than I'd ever imagined. The gun lobby misled a vocal minority of gun extremists to believe their guns will be taken away, but millions of moms are afraid our children will be taken away. We are fiercely and fearlessly taking on one of the most powerful lobbies this nation has ever seen—and we are winning" (Watts 2016).

Further Reading

Barron, James. 2013. "Gun Control Advocate Looking for a Million Good Moms." *New York Times,* January 20, 2013. https://cityroom.blogs.nytimes.com

/2013/01/20/gun-control-advocate-looking-for-a-million-good-moms
/?mtrref=www.google.com.

Kopel, Dave. 2014. "Not Watts She Seems." America's First Freedom, September
1, 2014. https://www.americas1stfreedom.org/articles/2014/9/1/not-watts
-she-seems/.

Watts, Shannon. 2016. "Four Years after Sandy Hook, Still Leading the Charge
for Stronger Gun Laws." Huffington Post, December 15, 2016. https://
www.huffingtonpost.com/entry/four-years-after-sandy-ho_b_13653656
.html.

Wemple, Erik. 2016. "NPR Issues Large Correction about Stay-at-Home Mom
/Gun Control Activist." *Washington Post,* June 23, 2016. https://www.wash
ingtonpost.com/blogs/erik-wemple/wp/2016/06/23/npr-issues-large
-correction-about-stay-at-home-momgun-control-activist/?utm_term
=.7a9f1c6298a9.

Woo, Michelle. 2018. "I'm Shannon Watts, Founder of Moms Demand Action for
Gun Sense in America, and This Is How I Parent." Lifehacker, June 4, 2018.
https://offspring.lifehacker.com/im-shannon-watts-founder-of-moms
-demand-action-for-gun-1826497811.

Further Resources

The Parkland Shooting and the Never Again Movement

Alter, Charlotte. 2018. "The School Shooting Generation Has Had Enough." *Time,* March 22, 2018. http://time.com/longform/never-again-movement/.

Arnold, Amanda. 2018. "The Most Powerful Moments from the March for Our Lives." The Cut, March 24, 2018. https://www.thecut.com/2018/03/march-for-our-lives-2018-the-most-powerful-moments.html.

Burrus, Trevor. 2018. "Let's Commit to Lowering Gun Deaths by 50 Percent in Ten Years. Will the Parkland Students' Proposals Help?" Cato Institute, March 27, 2018. https://www.cato.org/publications/commentary/lets-commit-lowering-gun-deaths-50-percent-ten-years-will-parkland-students.

Calvert, Scott. 2018. "Since Parkland's #NeverAgain, School Shootings Have Happened Again." *Wall Street Journal,* March 14, 2018. https://www.wsj.com/articles/since-parklands-neveragain-school-shootings-have-happened-again-1521019801.

Cottle, Michelle. 2018. "How Parkland Students Changed the Gun Debate." *The Atlantic,* February 28, 2018. https://www.theatlantic.com/politics/archive/2018/02/parkland-students-power/554399/.

Cullen, Dave. 2018. "'The News Forgets. Very Quickly.' Inside the Marjory Stoneman Douglas Students' Incredible Race to Make History." *Vanity Fair,* March 7, 2018. https://www.vanityfair.com/news/2018/03/inside-the-marjory-stoneman-douglas-students-race-to-make-history.

Editors of *The Lancet.* 2018. "#NeverAgain: Gun Violence and Youth Activism in America." *The Lancet,* March 1, 2018. https://www.thelancet.com/pdfs/journals/lanchi/PIIS2352–4642(18)30076-2.pdf.

Falkowski, Lisa, and Eric Garner, eds. 2018. *We Say #NeverAgain: Reporting by the Parkland Student Journalists.* New York: Crown Books for Young Readers.

Hogg, David, and Lauren Hogg. 2018. *#NeverAgain: A New Generation Draws the Line.* New York: Random House.

Howe, Neil. 2018. "#NeverAgain: A New Generation Takes Aim in the Gun Debate." *Forbes,* August 3, 2018. https://www.forbes.com/sites/neilhowe /2018/08/03/neveragain-a-new-generation-takes-aim-in-the-gun-debate /#69a611bb5718.

Lee, Elizabeth. 2018. "Parents, Students Fear Mass Shootings Now the New Normal in U.S." Voice of America, November 10, 2018. https://www.voanews .com/a/parents-students-fear-mass-shootings-now-the-new-normal -in-us/4652299.html.

Lopez, German. 2018. "Why the March for Our Lives Could Win." Vox, March 26, 2018. https://www.vox.com/policy-and-politics/2018/3/24/17158592 /march-for-our-lives-gun-control-nra.

March for Our Lives. 2018. https://marchforourlives.com/.

March for Our Lives Founders. 2018. *Glimmers of Hope: How Tragedy Sparked a Movement.* New York: Razorbill.

Miller, Lisa. 2018. "War Room." New York Magazine, March 5, 2018. http:// nymag.com/intelligencer/2018/03/on-the-ground-with-parkland -teens-as-they-plot-a-revolution.html?gtm=bottom&gtm=bottom.

"#NeverAgain." Brady Campaign to Prevent Gun Violence. http://www.brady campaign.org/neveragain.

Petrusich, Amanda. 2018. "The Fearless, Outraged Young Protesters at the March for Our Lives." *New Yorker,* March 24, 2018. https://www.newyorker .com/news/news-desk/the-march-for-our-lives-photographs-from -washington-dc.

"Student Voices: How Teens Want to Solve America's School Shooting Problem." 2018. PBS, March 8, 2018. http://www.pbs.org/newshour/extra/student -voices/how-teens-want-to-solve-americas-school-shooting-problem/.

Witt, Emily. 2018. "How the Survivors of Parkland Began the Never Again Movement." *New Yorker,* February 19, 2018. https://www.newyorker.com /news/news-desk/how-the-survivors-of-parkland-began-the-never -again-movement.

Wolfe, Rachel. 2018. "How a Post-Columbine Generation Views Gun Control." Vox, March 23, 2018. https://www.vox.com/policy-and-politics/2018 /2/20/17029880/gun-control-parkland-shooting-younger-americans.

Yee, Vivian, and Alan Blinder. 2018. "National School Walkout: Thousands Protest against Gun Violence across the U.S." *New York Times,* March 14, 2018. https://www.nytimes.com/2018/03/14/us/school-walkout.html.

Zornick, George. 2018. "How the #NeverAgain Movement Is Disrupting Gun Politics." *The Nation,* April 30, 2018. https://www.thenation.com/article /how-the-neveragain-movement-is-disrupting-gun-politics/.

Mass Shootings in America

Burns, Asia Simone. 2018. "Mass Shootings Spur Movements, but Gun Violence Is Constant for Some Americans." National Public Radio, April 10, 2018.

https://www.npr.org/2018/04/10/598821281/mass-shootings-spur-move
ments-but-gun-violence-is-constant-for-some-americans.

CNN Library. 2018. "Deadliest Mass Shootings in Modern U.S. History Fast Facts."
CNN, November 14, 2018. https://www.cnn.com/2013/09/16/us/20-dead
liest-mass-shootings-in-u-s-history-fast-facts/index.html.

Cox, John Woodrow, and Steven Rich. 2018. "Scarred by School Shootings."
Washington Post, March 25, 2018. https://www.washingtonpost.com
/graphics/2018/local/us-school-shootings-history/?utm_term=.311d4
c0661d5.

Cullen, Dave. 2009. *Columbine.* New York: Twelve.

Doherty, Carroll. 2013. "Did Newtown Really Change Public Opinion about
Gun Control?" CNN, December 6, 2013. http://globalpublicsquare.blogs
.cnn.com/2013/12/06/did-newtown-really-change-public-opinion
-about-gun-control/?iref=allsearch.

Ehrenfreund, Max, and Zachary A. Goldfarb. 2015. "Eleven Essential Facts
about Guns and Mass Shootings in the United States." *Washington Post,*
June 18, 2015. https://www.washingtonpost.com/news/wonk/wp/2015
/06/18/11-essential-facts-about-guns-and-mass-shootings-in-the-united
-states/?utm_term=.40a9b1fea5e8.

Fisher, Max, and Josh Keller. 2017. "What Explains U.S. Mass Shootings? International Comparisons Suggest an Answer." *New York Times,* November 7,
2017. https://www.nytimes.com/2017/11/07/world/americas/mass-shoot
ings-us-international.html?action=click&module=RelatedCoverage&pgt
ype=Article&region=Footer.

Follman, Mark, Gavin Aronsen, and Deanna Pan. 2018. "A Guide to Mass Shootings in America." *Mother Jones,* November 19, 2018. https://www.mother
jones.com/politics/2012/07/mass-shootings-map/.

Klarevas, Louis. 2016. *Rampage Nation: Securing America from Mass Shootings.*
Buffalo, NY: Prometheus Books, 2016.

Klebold, Sue. 2016. *A Mother's Reckoning: Living in the Aftermath of Tragedy.* New
York: Crown.

Klein, Jessie. 2012. *The Bully Society: School Shootings and the Crisis of Bullying in
America's Schools.* New York: New York University Press.

Lemieux, Frederic. 2016. "Six Things to Know about Mass Shootings in America." Scientific American, June 13, 2016. https://www.scientificamerican.
com/article/6-things-to-know-about-mass-shootings-in-america/.

Lysiak, Matthew. 2013. *Newtown: An American Tragedy.* New York: Gallery Books.

Schildkraut, Jaclyn. 2018. *Mass Shootings in America: Understanding the Debates,
Causes, and Responses.* Santa Barbara, CA: ABC-CLIO.

Sherman, Amy. 2018. "How Do We Prevent School Shootings?" PolitiFact, February 15, 2018. https://www.politifact.com/truth-o-meter/article/2018
/feb/15/how-do-we-prevent-school-shootings/.

The Gun Control/Gun Rights Debate

Bever, Lindsey. 2018. "This Is Our Lane: The NRA Told Doctors to Mind Their Own Business. Then a Man Shot Up a Hospital." *Washington Post,* November 20, 2018. https://www.washingtonpost.com/health/2018/11/20/this -is-our-lane-nra-told-doctors-mind-their-business-then-man-shot-up -hospital/?utm_term=.5570e03eca84.

Burnett, Doug. 2016. "Does Carrying a Pistol Make You Safer?" National Public Radio, April 12, 2016. https://www.npr.org/2016/04/12/473391286/does -carrying-a-pistol-make-you-safer.

Campbell, Donald J. 2019. *America's Gun Wars: A Cultural History of Gun Control in the United States.* Santa Barbara, CA: Praeger.

Charles, Patrick J. 2018. *Armed in America: A History of Gun Rights from Colonial Militias to Concealed Carry.* Buffalo, NY: Prometheus Books.

Cook, Philip J., and Kristin A. Goss. 2014. *The Gun Debate: What Everyone Needs to Know.* Oxford: Oxford University Press.

Cornell, Saul. 2006. "The Early American Origins of the Modern Gun Control Debate: The Right to Bear Arms, Firearms Regulation, and the Lessons of History." *Stanford Law and Policy Review,* June 2006. https://law.stan ford.edu/publications/early-american-origins-modern-gun-control -debate-right-bear-arms-firearms-regulation-lessons-history/.

Cornell, Saul. 2017. "Five Types of Gun Laws the Founding Fathers Loved." The Conversation, October 15, 2017. http://theconversation.com/five-types -of-gun-laws-the-founding-fathers-loved-85364.

Golshan, Tara. 2018. "The Gun Control Debate in Congress Is No Longer about Guns." Vox, March 8, 2018. https://www.vox.com/policy-and-politics /2018/3/8/17081154/gun-control-debate-congress-republicans.

Jancer, Matt. 2018. "Gun Control Is as Old as the Old West." *Smithsonian Magazine,* February 5, 2018. https://www.smithsonianmag.com/history/gun -control-old-west-180968013/.

Melzer, Scott. 2009. *Gun Crusaders: The NRA's Culture War.* New York: New York University Press.

Morgan, Thad. 2018. "The NRA Supported Gun Control When the Black Panthers Had the Weapons." History.com, March 22, 2018. https://www.his tory.com/news/black-panthers-gun-control-nra-support-mulford-act.

Mosher, Dave, and Skye Gould. 2018. "The Odds That a Gun Will Kill the Average American May Surprise You." Business Insider, October 29, 2018. https:// www.businessinsider.com/us-gun-death-murder-risk-statistics-2018-3.

Spitzer, Robert. 2015. *Guns across America: Reconciling Gun Rules and Rights.* Oxford: Oxford University Press.

Waldman, Michael. 2014. *The Second Amendment: A Biography.* New York: Simon and Schuster.

Watkins, Ali. 2018. "How the NRA Keeps Federal Gun Regulators in Check." *New York Times,* February 22, 2018. https://www.nytimes.com/2018/02 /22/us/politics/trump-atf-nra.html.

Webster, Daniel W., Cassandra K. Crifasi, Jon S. Vernick, and Alexander McCourt. 2017. "Concealed Carry of Firearms: Facts vs. Fiction." Johns Hopkins Bloomberg School of Public Health, Center for Gun Policy and Research, November 16, 2017. https://www.jhsph.edu/research/centers -and-institutes/johns-hopkins-center-for-gun-policy-and-research/publi cations/concealed-carry-of-firearms.pdf.

Whitney, Craig R. 2012. *Living with Guns: A Liberal's Case for the Second Amendment*. New York: PublicAffairs.

Wilson, Harry L. 2007. *Guns, Gun Control, and Elections*. Lanham, MD: Rowman and Littlefield.

Wilson, Harry L. 2016. *Gun Politics in America: Historical and Modern Documents in Context*. Santa Barbara, CA: ABC-CLIO.

Winkler, Adam. 2011. *Gunfight: The Battle over the Right to Bear Arms in America*. New York: Norton.

Index

Aaron Feis Guardian Act, 95
Abbott, Greg, 75
accidental shootings, risk of, 95
active shooter (term), 13
active-shooter drills
    growing up with, 67, 97, 127
    impact of, 7
    as normal routine, 116
    overview of, 58
    pros and cons, 92–93
    weariness of, 124
active-shooter incident, 3–4, 40, 95
active-shooter protocol, 36–37
African Americans, 54, 99
AK-47, 31
Alcorn, Ted, 114
Alter, Charlotte, 60
Amendment 777, 27
American Civil Liberties Union, 19
Americans for Responsible Solutions, 120
ammunition magazine sizes, restricting, 132
ammunition sales, legislation affecting, 26
antibullying policies, 75
Appelbaum, Paul, 16
Aquilino, John, 22
AR-15 semiautomatic rifle, 2, 31, 45, 46, 53, 55, 57, 63, 64, 85, 110, 125

"assault rifles" (term), 85
assault weapons ban, calls for, 6, 31, 32, 46, 63, 69, 85–87, 103, 113, 138
Aurura, Colo. movie theater shooting, 2012, 51, 139
Austin Police Department, 14
autism spectrum disorder, 47, 51
automatic weapons, 27, 28, 87
Avecedo, Art, 75
Azar, Alex, 79

background checks
    assault weapons ban versus, 86–87
    debates concerning, 30–31
    establishing, 60, 117
    expanding, 46, 48
    legislation promoting, 81–82
    opposition to, 82, 110
    prohibited persons, putting into system, 135
    push for, 38, 39–40, 120
    room for, 44
    strengthening, 113
    system, 51, 54
Baker, Jennifer, 80
Baptist church shooting, San Antonio, Tex., 2017, 6
Barber, Ron, 120

Barden, Daniel, 109–110, 111

Barden, Mark, 48, 109–111

#BlackLivesMatter, 97

Black Lives Matter movement, 98

Black Lives Matter protests, 137

Bloomberg, Michael, 48, 105, 112–115, 140, 141

Bloomberg LP, 113

bombs, 33–34

Book, Lauren, 116

boycotts, 99, 105

boyfriend loophole, 88

Brady, James, 29

Brady, Sarah, 29

Brady Campaign to Prevent Handgun Violence, 29, 44

Brady Center to Prevent Handgun Violence, 29

Brady Handgun Violence Prevention Act, 1993 (Brady Bill), 8, 29–31, 81–82, 103, 134

brain injury survivors, 119–120

Brauer, Jurgen, 6

Broward County Public Schools, 95

bump stocks, ban on, 56, 60, 87, 123

Bureau of Alcohol, Tobacco, Firearms, and Explosives (ATF)

    digitization of gun records kept by, 69, 80–81, 88

    gun legislation enforced by, 22, 25

    restrictions placed on, 26, 28, 29

Bush, George H. W., 134

Bush, George W., 40

Calderon, Alfonso, 63

campus-wide security alerts, 40, 58

Carter, Harlon B., 22–23, 24

Carter, Jimmy, 31

Casey, Mackenzie, 67

Cassidy, Warren, 28

Cato Institute, 42–43

Center for Peace Studies and Violence Prevention, 40

Centers for Disease Control and Prevention (CDC), 69, 79–80

Center to Prevent Handgun Violence, 29

Chadwick, Sarah, 63

Charleston, S.C., church shooting in, 52, 54

Chavez, Edna Lisbeth, 70

Chen, Alice, 78–79

children, preventing gun access by, 89

Cho, Seung Hui, 38–39, 40

church shootings, 52, 54, 55, 56, 82

Cicilline, David, 86

civil rights movement, 67, 71, 97, 98

Clinton, Bill, 29, 31, 85, 136

Clooney, George and Amal, 64, 68

Coetzee, J. M., 15

collateral damage, avoiding, 95

college and university campuses, debate over weapons on, 38, 40

college and university security measures, 40

Columbine (Cullen), 37

Columbine High School shooting, 1999

    admiration for perpetrators of, 38, 51

    armed personnel unable to prevent, 95

    books on, 97

    gun control organizations launched in wake of, 120

    gun rights defender response to, 135

    large-capacity magazines (LCMs) used in, 84

    Marjory Stoneman Douglas school shooting compared to, 57

    mass shootings after, 6

    overview of, 32–37

    public concern in wake of, 13, 66

    Santa Fe school shooting compared to, 73–74

    school safety since, 92–93

concealed carry, 94

concealed weapons, eliminating restrictions on, 5, 16–17
confiscation of guns
  digitized gun registration database role in, 80
  fear of, 22, 42
  opposition to, 4
  right to bear arms violated by, 86
  warnings of, 134
Congress on Your Corner, Tucson, Ariz., shooting at, 2018, 119
Conservative Political Action Conference, 137
conspiracy theories over shootings, 48–49, 53, 129–130, 132
consumer boycotts, 99, 105
copycat crimes, media role in, 37, 39
Corin, Jaclyn
  activist role, 131
  determination to be heard, 9
  on gun violence cycle, 66
  Kasky, C. march planning recalled by, 67–68
  at March for Our Lives protest, 70
  Never Again campaign joined by, 63
  photos, 64
  profile, 115–118
  on social media, 60
  Trump, D. criticized by, 75
Cornyn, John, 56
Cotton, Charles, 105
country music festival shooting, Las Vegas, Nev., 2017, 6, 52–56, 84, 102
Cox, Chris, 100
Crime Gun Tracing Modernization Act, 2018, 81
criminal background checks, 46, 51, 54, 60, 117
crisis actors, 59, 123, 129
crisis intervention training, 94
Crum, Allen, 15
Cruz, Nikolas, 57, 64
Cullen, Dave, 37, 97

Curry, Paige, 74

Dana (television show), 137
The Dana Show (radio show), 137
danger, perception of, 7
D'Avino, Rachel, 46
Day, Jerry, 15
death, gun violence as cause of, 78
death outside school, prevalence of, 93
death sentence, 54
death threats, 129, 132, 138
DeGeneres, Ellen, 117
Deitsch, Ryan, 63, 74, 95, 128
Democratic Party, 5, 20
Democrats, 95, 100
developed countries, 7
Dickey, Jay, 78, 79
Dickey Amendment, 78, 79
disaffected youth, outreach for, 66
District of Columbia v. Heller (2008), 5, 41–45
District of Columbia, 22, 42–44, 86
Dodd, Thomas J., 18, 19
domestic abusers, 88–89
domestic violence conviction, 56, 82
Dream Defenders, 99
drug addicts, 20, 25

Emanuel African Methodist Episcopal Church, Charleston, S.C., 54
Emergency Committee for Gun Control, 19, 20
emergency notification systems, 7
The Essential Second Amendment Guide (LaPierre), 134
Etsy, Elizabeth, 111
evacuation plans, 36
Everytown for Gun Safety, 69, 82, 104, 105, 114–115, 140, 141
Extreme Risk Protection Orders (ERPO), 51, 88

families of shooting victims, funds for, 69

family members, shooter killing of,
    14, 46
federal assault weapons ban, 31–32,
    62, 134
Federal Bureau of Investigation (FBI),
    3–4, 30, 54, 128, 138
Federal Firearms Act of 1938, 18, 20
Federal Firearms Licenses (FFLs), 25
federal gun control legislation, 24
federal lawmakers, gun control
    measures by, 17–18
federal license as gun industry
    requirement, 18
Feinstein, Dianne, 31, 32, 47
felons, 18, 20, 25, 29, 43
firearms, civilian use and misuse
    of, 43
firearms access, 88–89
Firearms Control Regulations Act,
    1975, 42, 43
Firearms Owners Protection Act
    (FOPA), 1986, 20, 24, 25–28, 80
firearms sales, shootings followed
    by, 6
firearms storage, 89
firearm transport, interstate, 26–27,
    87–88
First Baptist Church, Sutherland
    Springs, Tex., 55
Fix NICS Act, 56, 82–83
Florida, gun laws in, 55, 60
Florida, gun rights candidate victories
    in, 100
Florida State Capitol, Tallahassee,
    student trip to, 2018, 63
Ford, Gerald, 31
Fox, James Alan, 7, 93
Friedman, Dan, 80

Gabby (Kelly and Giffords), 120
Ganz, Marshall, 101
Garcia, Lily Eskelsen, 94
Gardiner, Avery, 44
Gardner, Neil, 34

gay nightclub shooting, Orlando,
    Fla., 2016, 6, 52, 54–55
Gibson, Leslie, 60
Giffords (gun control group), 100,
    104, 120
Giffords, Gabby, 104, 118–121
Glenn, John, 19
The Global War on Guns (LaPierre),
    134
Gluck, Larry, 36
González, Emma
    activist role, 68, 131
    critical references to, 60
    friends, 128
    grief, dealing with, 62
    gun debate, views on, 2
    at March for Our Lives protest, 71
    photos, 64
    social media used by, 99
    speeches, 59, 62, 71, 122, 123
government tyranny, firearms
    regulation as, 42
Grady, Chris, 105
Guillermo-Smith, Carlos, 55
Gumbel, Andrew, 33
gun control
    absolutist approach to measures
        for, 24
    candidate positions on, 99, 100
    debate over, 13, 18–19, 59, 87
    as Democratic Party priority, 5, 20
    impasse on, breaking through, 60
    laws and legislation, 1–2, 2–3,
        4, 24
    mass shootings followed by calls
        for, 6, 8, 50, 52, 66
    opposition to, 54
    shift in public views on, 65,
        102–106
    young activists advocating for, 99
Gun Control Act, 1968
    ATF created through, 80
    backlash against, 25
    NRA member views on, 23

overview of, 17–20
urban riots and public figure
assassinations, response to,
21–22
weakening of, 24, 26, 29
gun control advocates, 1, 38, 44–45
gun control amendment (to FOPA),
27–28
gun control rally, Broward County
Federal Courthouse, Fort
Lauderdale, Fla., 2018, 62
"gun dealer" (defined), 26, 114
gun dealers, legislation affecting,
25–26
gun-free zones, 94
gun industry, 18, 81
gun licenses
applications for, 56
industry requirements, 18
for purchase and ownership, 19,
20, 27
gun lobby, 1–2
gunmen, admiration for, 38
gunmen, media portrayal of, 34–35
gun owners
gun control efforts by, 120
gun violence, views on, 4
legislation favoring, 26–27
rights, protecting, 47
shootings, response to, 15, 55–56
gun ownership
ban on, 4–5, 42
as individual right, 4–5
licenses for, 19, 20
minimum age for, increasing, 62
restrictions on, 22, 47
United States and other countries
compared, 3
gun ownership registry, national, 19,
24, 26, 27
gun purchase license, 27
gun purchases, minimum age for, 117,
132, 138
gun registration, 19, 20, 42, 80–81

gun-related crimes, solving, 80
gun-related homicides and suicides,
22
gun rights, expansion of, 5
gun rights advocates
assault weapons ban opposed by,
86
gun control legislation, concerns
over, 22
gun control legislation resisted by,
50, 52, 66
Heller court ruling, interpretation
of, 44
political activism by, 103
school shootings, response to, 38,
66
Second Amendment as viewed by, 1
gun rights extremists, 59–60
gun sale and registration records,
digitizing, 69, 80–81, 88, 103
gun sales, illegal, difficulty of
uncovering, 28
gun shows, firearms sales at, 4, 26
gun tracing, 81, 88
gun trafficking, 87–88
Gun Trafficking Prevention Act, 88
gun violence
breaking cycle of, 59, 65
as cause of death, 78
causes of, 1, 87–89, 111
as common occurrence, 139
demonstration against, 61
epidemic of, 1
exposure to, 93
growing up with, 127, 139
marching against, 69–71 (*see also*
March for Our Lives protest,
2018)
measures to reduce, 105
political inaction on, impatience
over, 106
prevalence of, 1, 3, 58
protecting communities against,
113

gun violence (*cont.*)
  raising awareness over, 132
  reductions in, 83
Gun Violence Archive, 3
gun violence prevention
  campaign aimed at, 135
  debate over, 38, 77, 138
  hearings on, 111
  impasse over, 13
  measures, 7, 13, 35–36, 120, 126
gun violence prevention movement, 57
gun violence research, 63, 69, 78–80
gun violence victims, 87, 117

Handgun Control, Inc., 29
handguns
  acquiring, prohibition on, 22
  concealed, 16–17
  interstate shipment, ban on, 18
  sales, waiting period for, 30
Hands Off My Gun (Loesch), 137
Hardy, David, 26, 27
Harper-Mercer, Chris, 50
Harris, Eric, 33–34, 35
Harsanyi, David, 71
hate crimes, 54
hate groups, 54
Heller, Dick, 43
Hernandez, Daniel, 119
high-capacity magazines, 42, 62,
  63, 69
Hinckley, John, Jr., 29
Hochsprung, Dawn, 46
Hockley, Dylan, 125, 126
Hockley, Ian, 125
Hockley, Jake, 125, 126
Hockley, Nicole, 48, 94, 125–127
Hogg, David
  activist role, 68, 131
  on challenges to student movement,
    63, 100
  critical references to, 60
  on elected official accountability,
    64–65, 99

on fear, 58
photos, 64
on politicians, 4
profile, 128–130
social media used by, 99
speeches, 62
Hogg, Kevin, 128
Hogg, Lauren, 128, 129, 130
homicides, 18–19, 22
HONR Network, 49
House Resolution 5087, 86
Huckabee, Mike, 51
Hughes, William J., 27

individual citizens, Second
  Amendment and, 42
Ingraham, Laura, 60
Institute for Legislative Action (ILA),
  22, 26, 28
International Association of Chiefs
  of Police, 19
ISIS (Islamic State of Iraq and
  Syria), 55

Johnson, Lyndon B., 18, 19, 20
Jones, Alex, 49

Kaine, Tim, 40
Kasky, Cameron
  as activist, 62, 129
  March for Our Lives idea attributed
    to, 67–68
  at March for Our Lives protest, 70
  Never Again MSD cofounded by, 117
  photos, 64
  profiles, 130–133
  Sandy Hook parent, meeting
    with, 127
  social media used by, 99
Kasky, Holden, 131
Kasky, Jeff, 130–131
Kelley, Devin Patrick, 55
Kelly, Mark, 119, 120
Kelly, Zaire, 70

Kelly, Zion, 70
Kennedy, John F., 18
Kennedy, Robert, 18
King, Martin Luther, Jr., 18, 70, 98
King, Yolanda Renee, 70, 98
Klebold, Dylan, 33–34, 35
Knox, Neal, 23

Lankford, Adam, 73
Lanza, Adam, 46–47, 126
Lanza, Nancy, 46
LaPierre, Wayne, 48, 133–135, 137
La Porte, Barbara, 40
large-capacity magazines (LCMs)
  ban sought for, 32, 47, 56,
    83–85, 86
  defined, 83
Las Vegas shooting, 2017, 6, 52–56,
    84, 102
Lavergne, Gary, 13
Law Center to Prevent Gun
    Violence, 120
law enforcement personnel, 94
law enforcement response to crisis
    situations, 13, 14–15, 36–37
Leahy, Patrick, 81
legal guns, shooting with, 46, 51,
    74, 131
Levinson, Meira, 97
Levy, Robert, 42–43
Lewis v. United States (1980), 20
Lithwick, Dahlia, 45
lockdown drills, 36, 67, 92, 97
Loesch, Chris, 136
Loesch, Dana, 122–123, 136–138
Lopez, German, 2, 42, 103, 104
Loughner, Jared Lee, 119

machine guns, 18, 27, 28
Maddow, Rachel, 117
Magaw, John, 30
mail-order ammunition, 26
mail-order guns, 18, 20
Manchin-Toomey Amendment, 110

mandatory waiting periods, 60, 117
March for Our Lives organization,
    132
March for Our Lives protest, 2018
  demands and impact, 77–89, 118
  National Rifle Association response
    to, 8
  Never Again movement
    culminating in, 13
  overview of, 66–71
  planning and organizing, 63, 64,
    74, 114–115, 123, 131–132
  public opinion shift, role in, 105
  reach of message at, 102
  shootings following, 73
  speakers at, 98, 117
  turnout, 2, 57, 61
  in youth activism age, 96–97
Marjory Stoneman Douglas (MSD)
    High School shooting, Parkland,
    Fla., 2018
  aftermath and outcome, 66–67,
    121–124, 137, 138, 141
  armed personnel unable to
    prevent, 95
  assault weapon used in, 85
  as commonplace incident, 7, 116
  gun rights defender response
    to, 135
  interviews during, 128–129
  large-capacity magazines (LCMs)
    used in, 83, 84
  overview of, 57–61
  preventing another, 91
  Sandy Hook parent reaction to,
    126–127
  school and other shootings before,
    93, 102
  survivors (*see* Parkland shooting
    survivors)
Martin, Trayvon, 99
Martinez, Ramiro, 15
mass murder (defined), 13
mass shooters, idolizing of, 50

mass shooters, law enforcement engagement with, 36–37

mass shooting generation
determination to be heard, 9
experiences of, 58
mobilizing, 67
perception of danger among, 7
school shootings, reaction to, 74
self-described, 97
term, 2

mass shootings
deadliest, 52, 54, 135
and demands for action, 5–7, 24
large-capacity magazines (LCMs) used in, 83–84
NRA popularity decline following, 105
psychological and emotional impact of, 4
public concerns over, 1
response, debate over, 51
semiautomatic firearms used in, 31
statistics, 3
term, 13

Mateen, Omar, 54, 55
mayors, 113
Mayors Against Illegal Guns, 114, 140
McCoy, Houston, 15
McDonald v. City of Chicago, 44
McVeigh, Timothy, 134–135
media coverage of shootings, 15, 33, 37
mental health care, 33, 54, 66, 135
mental illness, violence linked to, 16
mentally ill. *See* people with mental illness
metal detectors, 36, 75, 92
#MeToo movement, 97, 98
midterm elections, 2018, 9, 64–65, 100, 104, 124, 130
military, discharge from, 56, 82
military-style weapons, ban on, 31, 46, 85–87, 113
militias, 41, 42, 43
millennials of voting age, 2, 100

minority children from impoverished urban areas, 87
minors, gun sales prohibited to, 20, 25
Mintz, Chris, 50
"modern sporting rifles" (term), 85
Moms Demand Action for Gun Sense in America, 6, 114, 140–141
Morales, Ed, 98
Mothers Against Drunk Driving, 140
MSD High School Public Safety Act, 60, 63–64, 117
Murphy, Anne Marie, 46, 125

National Association of School Resource Officers (NASRO), 95
National Center for Education Statistics, 92
National Education Association, 94
National Firearms Act of 1934, 18, 19–20, 27, 79
National Instant Criminal Background Check System (NICS)
creation of, 30, 81–82
data missing from, 56
strengthening measures, 39–40, 56, 82–83
National Institutes of Health, 79
National Rifle Association (NRA)
on armed defenders in schools, 94
assault weapons ban opposed by, 86
automatic weapons restrictions, views on, 28
background checks opposed by, 82, 110
Brady Bill fought by, 29
businesses pressured to sever ties to, 60, 99, 105
campaign contributions from, 62, 65, 97, 100, 129, 132
Cincinnati revolt, 21–24
contributions to, 103

declining influence of, 104–106
extreme, hardline approach, 5, 41
Gun Control Act, 1968 impact
on, 25
gun control legislation opposed by,
1–2, 4, 6, 18, 19, 91
historic overview, 20
large-capacity magazines (LCMs)
ban opposed by, 84
leader profiles, 133–135
lobbying arm, 22, 26, 28
membership increase, 20, 24, 134
political alignments, 5, 24, 42
political influence, counteracting,
2, 62, 64, 68, 99, 117, 135,
137, 140
as political lobbying force, 4, 5, 13
school shootings, response to,
24, 48
shift into politics, 20, 25
spokesperson profiles, 136–138
student anger toward, 7–8, 9,
59, 62
student gun control activists
criticized by, 8
National School Walkout, 7, 61,
93, 117
National Tracing Center, 80, 81
Nelson, Bill, 81, 122
#NeverAgain, 99, 117, 127, 131,
135, 137
#Never Again (Hogg), 130
Never Again movement
gun rights supporters critical of, 8
gun violence research as priority
of, 79
launch of, 13, 57, 62–63, 102, 123
overview of, 2, 61–65
political power of, 104
Never Again MSD, 8, 63, 64,
68, 117
NICS Improvement Act, 40
non-gun owners, views on gun
violence, 4

NRA Political Victory Fund, 100,
105–106

Obama, Barack
gun control, public opinion during,
47, 113
gun control legislation, call for, 46,
48, 54
Parkland students, correspondence
with, 64
Sandy Hook parents, meetings
with, 111
on thoughts and prayers, 50
on youth activism, 97
Obama, Michelle, 64
Obbie, Mark, 44
of underprivileged backgrounds, 117
Oklahoma City bombing, 1995,
33, 134
Omero, Margie, 105
Omnibus Safe Streets and Crime
Control Act, 1968, 18
One Million Moms for Gun Control,
140
online, firearm sales conducted, 48
oppressed peoples, 23
organized crime, 18
Orth, Franklin, 21, 22
Oswald, Lee Harvey, 18

Paddock, Stephen, 53
Pagourtzis, Dimitrios, 73–74
panic buttons in classrooms, 75
Parkland shooting survivors
activism and impact of, 7–9, 66–71,
96, 102–103
discussions with, 132, 138
Everytown for Gun Safety aid to,
114–115
gun reform movement led by, 2,
58–61, 102–103
Never Again movement launched
by, 13
organizing by, 62–63

Parkland shooting survivors (*cont.*)
  profiles, 115–118, 121–124,
    128–133
  Sandy Hook parent appreciation
    toward, 111
  Santa Fe High School shooting,
    reaction to, 74–75
Parsons, Chelsea, 5
people with drug addictions, 20, 25
people with mental illness
  background checks for, 38, 39–40
  gun possession prohibited to, 43
  gun purchases prohibited to, 20,
    25, 60, 103, 117
  guns obtained by, 29, 51, 54
  school shootings by, 35, 47, 50, 64
Perry, Bruce D., 93
Plenzler, Joe, 85
Poleshook, Melanie, 36
police
  in schools, 48, 60
  state control of, 17
  tactics, 33
  training, 16
  warning signs of shooting, 138
political action committee, 8, 67, 68
potentially violent people, gun
    purchases prohibited to, 60,
    117
Pozner, Leonard, 49
Pozner, Noah, 49
Pratt, Erich, 40
presidential election, 2020, 100
price of freedom, gun violence as, 6,
    7, 74
private gun sale loophole, 82, 83
prohibited groups of people, 20, 25,
    88–89, 135
public carry, prohibitions on, 44
public figures, assassination of, 16, 18
public opinion shift, 8, 105
public reaction to shootings, 1, 13,
    15–16, 47
public safety, state control of, 17

Public Safety and Recreational
    Firearms Use Protection Act,
    31–32, 62, 110
Pulse gay nightclub shooting,
    Orlando, Fla., 2016, 54–55

race and gun violence
  victimization, 87
racial justice, movement for, 98
Reagan, Ronald, 26, 29, 31
red flag laws, 88
Republican Party, 5, 20, 24, 42
Republicans on arming teachers, 95
resource officers, 94, 95, 97
restaurants and retail chains, guns
    prohibited in, 141
Rich, Maxwell, 22
right to bear arms, 5, 22, 86
right-wing media personalities, 59–60
Road to Change tour, 99
Roof, Dylann, 54
Roosevelt, Franklin D., 18
Rousseau, Lauren, 46
Route 91 Harvest Festival, 52–53
Rubio, Marco, 51–52, 71, 122, 132

Safarik, Mark, 114
Sanders, Dave, 34, 36
Sandy Hook Elementary School
    shooting, 2012
  activism in wake of, 139, 140
  admiration for perpetrator of, 51
  aftermath and outcome of, 6
  assault weapons ban efforts
    after, 32
  death toll from, 93
  growing up with, 58
  gun rights defender response to, 135
  gun violence causes, attempt to
    resume studies after, 79
  large-capacity magazines (LCMs)
    used in, 84
  NRA membership increase
    following, 24

opinion pieces written after, 113
overview of, 45–49
parent response to, 110
public response in wake of, 13
response to, 66
survivors, 67
Sandy Hook Promise, 6, 48, 94, 110, 111, 126
Santa Fe High School shooting, 2018, 73–75
school safety, policy changes involving, 33
school security measures
advocacy of, 66
impact of, 7
implementing, 36
negative impact of, 91–92, 93
proposals, 77
school shootings
armed resource officers unable to prevent, 95
deadliest, 38, 45–46, 57
increase in, 16
NRA response to, 24
prevalence of, 91, 93, 114
psychological damage caused by, 93
public concern over, 13
United States and other countries compared, 7
school staff members, arming, 60
school violence, growing up with, 127
Schultz, Debbie Wasserman, 116
Scott, Rick, 55, 98–99
Second Amendment
absolutist interpretation of, 24, 41–42, 134
activists, 23
candidates supporting, 103
gun rights supporter views on, 1, 4, 71, 75, 79, 86
gun safety *versus,* 120
interpretation, shift in, 41–42
lower court rulings on, 22

NRA interpretation of, 19, 28, 41–42, 91
Parkland student activism *versus,* 71, 105
state laws to protect, 55
Supreme Court rulings affecting, 5, 20, 41, 42, 43–44, 45
text, 41
votes in support of, 100, 103
security cameras, 97
security guards, armed, 36, 46, 94, 135
self-defense, 55, 56, 100
semiautomatic assault weapons
accessories enhancing, 87
ban on, 31, 47
debates over, 138
firing rate, increasing, 60
restrictions on, 28, 84
semiautomatic firearms, 31–32, 48, 85
sensitive places, carrying firearms in, 43
serial numbers, 20
sexual assault, movement against, 98
Sherlach, Mary, 46
shooter profiles, 50, 51, 111, 126
shooters, messages from, 51
shootings, firearms sales following, 6
shootings, preventive measures, 7, 35–36, 126
Shufeldt, Greg, 67
A Sniper in the Room (Lavergne), 13
social change, 67, 98
socially isolated persons, shooting by, 50, 51, 111
social media
posting feelings on, 116
student accounts, monitoring, 75
student organizing on, 57, 59–60, 63, 99
social media-driven campaigns, 97
social upheaval of 1960s, 16, 18, 21, 71, 97
Spielberg, Steven, 64, 68

Spitzer, Robert, 27, 28, 59, 83,
    105–106
sportsmen, views on gun legislation, 21
stand-your-ground statute, 55, 99
Stevens, John Paul, 43
stores, guns prohibited in, 141
straw purchases, preventing, 88
Student Nonviolent Coordinating
    Committee, 98
Students, Teachers, and Officers
    Preventing (STOP) School
    Violence Act, 2018, 93–94
student safety, measures to increase, 75
Students Demand Action for Gun
    Sense in America, 115, 141
students of color, 87, 117
suicide
    gun-related, drop in, 22
    preventing, 88
    by shooters, 34, 46, 50, 53, 56, 73
Sutherland Springs, Tex., church
    shooting in, 52, 56
SWAT (special weapons and tactics)
    teams, 16, 36

talk show host profiles, 136–138
Tarr, Delaney
    activist role, 68, 131
    friends, 128
    at March for Our Lives protest, 70
    speeches, 62
    students' motivations described
        by, 63
    student's need for help
        acknowledged by, 69
teachers, arming, 77, 91, 93–95
terrorism, 58
terrorist attacks, 54–55
terrorists, suspected, guns purchased
    by, 55
terrorist watch list, 55
"thoughts and prayers" in response
    to shootings, 7, 50, 59, 62, 66,
    75, 106

threat-assessment teams, college use
    of, 40
Tiahrt, Todd, 81
Tiahrt Amendment, 81
Trump, Donald
    bump stock sales prohibition
        planned by, 87
    criticism of, 75
    Fix NICS Act signed by, 56, 83
    Sandy Hook parents, meetings
        with, 111
    school security focus by, 93
    teacher arming favored by, 94
    "thoughts and prayers" offered by, 62
tyrannical government, arms as
    defense against, 4

Umpqua Community College
    shooting, 2016, 50–52, 114
underprivileged background, 117
Underwood, Akeal, 70
Underwood, Christopher, 70
United States v. Warin (1976), 22
universal background checks
    call for, 31, 62, 63, 69, 81–83, 114
    presidential calls for, 6
    public views on, 4
University of Texas tower shooting,
    1966, 13–17
U.S. Chamber of Commerce, 19
U.S. Supreme Court
    background checks, rulings
        affecting, 30
    on Gun Control Act
        constitutionality, 20
    Second Amendment, rulings
        affecting, 5, 20, 41, 42, 43–44, 45

video games, violent, 66
Vietnam-era antiwar movement, 67,
    71, 97, 98
viewpoints, understanding different,
    132–133
vigilantism, 15

violence, mental illness linked to, 16
violence, random acts of, 13
violent crime, 18
Violent Crime Control and Law Enforcement Act, 1994, 31, 84, 85–86
violent youths, potential, outreach for, 66
Virginia Tech shooting, 2017, 38–40, 66, 135
Virginia Tech Victims Family Outreach Foundation, 40
Volpe, John Della, 100
voter registration, 98
voting power, 2–3
vulnerability, sense of, 13, 54

Wadler, Naomi, 70
Warner, Mark, 86
warning signs of shooting, 88, 111, 126, 137, 138
Watts, John, Jr., 139
Watts, Shannon, 139–141
"weapons of war" (term), 85

Welner, Michael, 39
white supremacists, 54
white supremacy, 137
Whitman, Charles, 13–14, 15, 16
Whitney, Sofie, 62, 127, 131
Willeford, Stephen, 55
Williams, Claire, 14
Wind, Alex, 62, 64, 131
Winfrey, Oprah, 64, 68
Winkler, Adam, 44
women, gun violence, protection from, 89
women, murders of, 88
Women's March, 137
Women's March organizers, 69
Women's March youth groups, 61

young voters
    campaign to register, 8–9, 62, 97, 99, 103, 124, 132
    impact of, 101
    mobilizing, 57, 64, 99–101
youth activism, 96–101

zero-tolerance policies, 35–36

About the Author

Laurie Collier Hillstrom is a freelance writer and editor based in Brighton, Michigan. She is the author of more than 40 books in the areas of American history, biography, and current events. Some of her previously published works include *The #MeToo Movement, Black Lives Matter: From a Moment to a Movement, Defining Moments: The Constitution and the Bill of Rights,* and *Defining Moments: The Stonewall Riots.*